IN ENGLISH

DESCRIPTIVE

GUIDEBOOK TO
CHICHEN ITZA
UP-DATED - EASY - COMPLETE

PROFR. GUALBERTO ZAPATA ALONZO

FIFTH EDITION IN ENGLISH

Author Address:
Calle 19 No. 137
Telephone 291395
Jardines Miraflores
Mérida, Yuc. México 97168.

ACKNOWLEDGEMENT

I sincerely wish to thank Ms. Eta Trabimg, a translator
and interpreter from Huston, Texas for her work in
the translation of this book. Without the assistance
of this fine lady, this book could not have been
published in this way in its English version.

TABLE OF CONTENTS

PROLOGUE

The author, hoping to provide visitors with an up-dated, easy and complete descriptive guidebook on the most important aspects in the history, monuments and sites of the archeologically fascinating Chichén Itzá, carefully took into consideration the best historical and archeological sources available, studying them in great detail so as to approximate as much as possible, the living conditions of the ancient, great Maya people in this region. They left us an inheritance of exquisite art and architecture, reflected in their magnificent sculptures, paintings, ceramics, and impressive monuments, which never cease to amaze nationals and foreigners alike, particularly in view of the era in which these were conceived and the tools they had to work with.

So that this guidebook may be easily understood by all, the language has been kept as simple and clear as possible, eliminating unnecesary details and technicalities, but keeping the flavor and sequence of the historical descriptions.

Notwithstanding the above, this work is somewhat more extensive than other descriptive guidebooks, because our aim has been to not leave visitors in doubt as to certain pertinent aspects.

We wish to take this opportunity to honor one of the most renowned historians of our country the late Juan Francisco Molina Solis, who with incredible patience, described the history of the Maya from its beginnings to its ultimate downfall in his magnificent, three-volume work entitled **Historia del Descubrimiento y Conquista de Yucatán** (History of the Discovery and Conquest of Yucatán) which took almost 50 years to write. He obtained permission from the Department of the Indies in Spain, to go through the archives in Seville, at the Escorial and in Simancas, where he was able to unearth valuable information practically unobtainable elsewhere. These very valuable reports had been sent to the Spanish gobernment by the town councils and "encomenderos" (holders of Spanish land grants) of Yucatán after the conquest, and by others that had actively participated in public life at the time of colonization. Molina Solis also obtained data from the chronicles written in the Maya language but phonetically transcribed into Spanish script.

No other history book on this region has been better written or contains more information. Molina Solis did not limit himself to simply obtaining data and recording it in a sequential manner; instead, when he encountered discrepancies in the narratives, he found the way to logically make them fi into the data that were generally accepted.

Other interesting data on Chichen Itza can be found in a book entitled **People of the Serpent.** Its author, Edward Herbert Thompson, was Vice-Consul for the United States of America in Yucatán during the early 20th century. Thompson purchased, at a very good price, the Chichén Itzá "hacienda", which the conquistadores had built whit the stones of the ruined Maya buildings. After acquiring the property, he proceeded, at his own cost and hiring both foreign and national divers, to drag and explore the Sacred Cenote; he also explored the Osario or Tomb of the High Priest and other important buildings.

Between 1925 and 1931, the building known as the Caracol or Observatory was restored, with the sponsorship of the Carnegie Institution of Washington, D.C., and under the direction of Karl Ruppert, among others.

Shortly after the work was finished, Karl Ruppert described the restoration process of this structure in his marvellously comprehensive book El Caracol, which was elegantly printed with more than 290 photographs, plus numerous maps and drawings.

One of the most extensive quidebooks of Chichén Itzá was written by the late Yucatecan archeologist, Manuel Cirerol Sansores, who dedicated many years of his life to researching and studying the areas around Chichén Itzá and Uxmal; and although his concepts were not generally accepted, his work, nevertheless, had many positive aspects.

It was Román Piña Chan, writer and archeologist, who described in great detail the results of the last two explorations of the Sacred Cenote, carried out in 1960-61 and 1967-68, in his 1970 Preliminary Report, published by the National Institute of Anthropology and History of the Mexican Ministry of Public Education. Piña Chan not only observed the work actually done there at the time, but was one of its principal directors.

The reader will now be aware that the above mentioned authors and explorers are undoubtedly the best that can be consulted with respect to the historical panorama of the Maya people; however, this does not preclude the fine work done by other scientists and researchers whose names and consulted works are listed in the Bibliography at the end of this book.

The writing, presentation, analyses and personal conclusions are the author's, who has dedicated almost 20 years to studying and investigating the many aspects of this incredible Maya culture, in hopes that his efforts will be useful to others.

8

GEOGRAPHIC LOCATION

Chichén Itzá is a well-known archeological site, nationally and internationally recognized for the beauty and splendor of its impressive monuments. The promotion of this site by the Mexican authorities has obviously been successful as more than 300,000 people visit it every year. It is located 120 kms east-southeast of the city of Mérida, capital of the state of Yucatán, along Highway 180, which continues to the Caribbean side of the Peninsula and such towns as Cancún, Puerto Juárez, Puerto Morelos, Playa del Carmen, Akumal, Xel-Há, the Maya ruins of Tulum, with a side road leading to the ruins of Cobá. From Tulum, it is easy to drive to Chetumal, capital of the state of Quintana Roo. Driving back to Mérida, you may wish to stop and visit the lovely lake of Bacalar, and Carrillo Puerto, then continue through the villages of Peto, Tzucacab, Tekax, Akil, :Oxkuzcab Ticul, Muna and Umán, to return to Mérida in Yucatán.

HOW TO GET THERE

There are various ways to get to Chichén Itzá; the first, and easiest, is to make arrangements with any of the many travel agencies located in Mérida. They will provide transportation services, a guide authorized by the Ministry of Tourism, admission tickets to the archeological site, and lunch, if you want it. There are two rates: one for a private, air-conditioned car, and the other for group service in a bus or van.

You can also go on your own, using the first or second-class bus services, with regularly scheduled departure times. The first-class bus service is non-stop and with assigned seating. Tickets must be purchased ahead of time at the bus terminal (Unión de Camioneros de Yucatán), located on Street 69, between Streets 68 and 70. The trip lasts one hour and 40 minutes. The second-class buses are almost always overcrowded, with many passengers having to stand; the trip takes about two hours.

If driving either your own or a rented car, the easiest way to get out of the city is along Street 59 Oriente (east) to where it ends and connects with the outer freeway loop; turn right and cross the paved highway to Tixkokob; turn left on to the next highway, which is No. 180.

This highway will take you past many henequen (Mexican sisal or agave) haciendas and typical Yucatecan villages. The haciendas are: San Pedro, Teya, Ticopó, San Bernardino and Holactún, all of which produce sisal fiber; the villages are Tahmek, Hoctún, Xocchel, Kantunil, Holca, Libre Unión, Yokdzonot and Pisté. Some months ago, the construction of a four-lane highway was started; when finished it will bypass some of the villages and make the trip easier and faster.

On the outskirts of Tahmek, you will find the Francisco Villa sisal shredding operation, where you can stop and watch the shredding of the agave plant leaves by means of an ingenious machine invented by Yucatecans. In seconds, this machine converts the green leaves into a white and resistant fiber that is packed in bales of 190 kgs. The sisal fiber is used to make cord for tying sheaves, ropes of various thicknesses, fiber rugs and many other curios.

TRIP DURATION

If you wish to make only a one-day trip, it takes about 3 1/2 hours there and back, road time; the actual visit to the archeological site lasts from 2 1/2 to 3 hours, plus one hour or so for lunch, for a total trip time of about 7 1/2 to 8 hours.

Those who wish to stay longer and see the monuments at leisure, can stay at the hotels close to the site, or in the village of Pisté, about two kilometers away. The hotels usually provide their guests with vehicles to and from the archeological site. These hotels and inns are classified as first, second and third class, and their rates vary accordingly.

CLIMATE AND APPROPRIATE CLOTHING

There are two tourist seasons: the first covers July and August, the regular summer vacation months in many countries around the world; the second runs from early December to mid-April. From mid-April to the end of August, the weather is hot. The rainy season starts in the latter half of May and goes through September. The rains are generally quite heavy ocurring once, twice or more times a week, almost always in the afternoons, and lasting from 15 minutes to two hours; occasionally, drizzle may continue for quite some time. Light clothing and a raincoat are advisable during this time of the year.

From September to December, storms in the Caribbean are common and bring intermittent rain and drizzle during the day and part of the night. From December to February, we suggest a sweater for the early mornings and late evenings. Bothersome insects are seldom a problem.

For those visitors who wish to go on their own, an authorized guide can be contracted at the archeological site offices, located at the ticket booth. These guides charge the rate authorized by the Tourism Office, and although they take turns, the visitor may select the guide that he/she prefers.

Children under 12, of any nationality, may enter free. Mexican students with proper credentials may also enter at no charge.

Because two substructures and one other building are only open at certain times, visitors should check the schedule posted at the ticket office.

Inside the buildings, it is forbidden to use a flash, a tripod, or a 16 or 35 mm movie camera, or to make tracings of the reliefs. To use a tripod or to be allowed to make tracings, you must obtain a permit from the National Institute of Anthropology and History and pay the respective fee; this can be done at the ticket office where you will be issued a receipt.

GENERAL INFORMATION

No one knows the origin of the Mayas, or of the different groups th populated the American continent in the early ages of man results of stud carried out so far rest only upon speculation.

Originally, it was believed that Amerindians came to this contine from Asia, around 15 to 20 thousand years before Christ, crossing the B ing Strait to Alaska; subsequent studies, however, place this migration 35 thousand years before Christ; some scientists indicate even earlier tim The Amerindians migrated in many different directions, and much later few reached what is now known as the Maya region.

In Mexican territory, this Maya region includes five states: portions Chiapas and Tabasco, and all of Campeche, Yucatán and Quintana Ro Outside the Mexican borders, it includes almost all of Guatemala, and p tions of El Salvador, Honduras and Belize, for an approximate total surfa area of 325,000 square kilometers, as shown on the map below.

Map of the Maya Region

12

Until quite recently, scientists believed that the advent of man in the
ya region, particularly in Honduras, Guatemala and neighboring areas,
:urred around 3000 B.C., and that the first human settlements began
und 800 B.C. Subsequent research, however, changed the date to 1500
:., and in 1976, primitive constructions of gypsum and mud were dis-
/ered in Belize. Charcoal found inside these buildings was subsequently
ntified as dating from 2500 B.C.

Just four years ago (May 12, 1980). Dr. Richard S. MacNeish, Arche-
gy Director for the Robert S. Peabody Foundation of Andover, Massa-
ssets, published findings on the remains of more than sixty fishing vil-
es that had existed along the Caribbean coast in about 6500 B.C. Even
re remarkable, however, was the discovery of part of a tusk, a molar and
bula of a mastodon, together with the hoof of a Pleistocene horse, 80
s tall, and bones of other prehistoric animals, found in chamber number
, named "Huechil", a section of the interesting and beautiful grottos of
tún, 7 kms from the village of Oxkutzcab and 110 kms south of Méri-
Yucatán. Loltún, in Maya, means "stone flower". According to arche-
gists of the Mexican National Institute of Anthropology and History
N.A.H.) in. charge of the excavations, these bones were associated with
ic tools that indicate man's presence in that area since 8000 B.C. or ear-
, which radically changes our previous thinking.

According to their particular points of view, experts classify and subdi-
e the evolutionary periods of the Maya Culture in different ways. The
st popular and accepted version, however, is the one put forth by the
lliant British archeologist, Eric S. Thompson, particularly with respect
the time between the Classic Period and the ultimate downfall of the
ya Culture.

Taking into account that village type agriculture started around 2500
:., a new classification table might be more appropriately restructured as
ows:

FIRST PERIOD: **Pre-Maya.** From time immemorial to 2500 B.C.
SECOND PERIOD: **Formative or Preclassic.** From 2500 B.C.
            to A.D. 200
THIRD PERIOD: **Classic.** Subdivided into three stages:
Early Classic. from A.D. 200 to 625 Flourishing Classic from A.D.
  625 to 800
Decadent Classic. from A.D. 800 to 925
FOURTH PERIOD: **Mexicaa or Toltec.** From A.D. 925 to 1200.
FIFTH PERIOD: **Mexican Absorption.** (Decadent Postclassic)
            from A.D. 1200 to 1540

Very little is known of the Formative Period; there are no historical data
elp in the research. What little information does exist has come mostly

from stratigraphic studies and speculative deductions by experts on the subject. Radioactive carbon-14 dating, which acts only on organic materials, is now being used extensively to aid these research processes.

In the process of exploring and excavating, archeologists analyze such objects as stone tools, clay. bones and other related materials, so as to establish a time of existence. This research has shown that around 2500 B.C., man's cultural development started with the construction of huts made of perishable materials, village agriculture began, tools were fashioned of hard stone, ceramics appeared, and religious ceremonies and rites came into being. Subsequently, letters and numerals were invented, writing began and the calendar was instituted. The process for making lime was discovered; the mixing of lime, at a ratio of 3:1, with the white earth called "sascab" or "sahcab" produced the mortar that gave rise to a more sophisticated architecture. All these advances constitute the foundations of the Classic Period.

During this most brilliant Classic Period, the Mayas attained their highest cultural levels. They built their most beautiful buildings, sculpted their most remarkable works and produced admirably elegant ceramics. Around A.D. 800, however, their decline began. They started to abandon their ceremonial centers one by one, starting in the central region and finally reaching portions of the northern region, known today as the "Puuc". This has left the impression that these Mayas disappeared from the cultural scene due to unexplained causes. Various possibilities have been considered: epidemics; crop losses for several years in succession due to declining soil conditions and prolonged droughts; invasions by savage tribes; earthquakes; and lastly, a rebellion by the people against the reigning nobles.

Some time after this decline, the Toltec influence, originating in Tula, began to appear in the northern part of the Yucatan Peninsula.

Tula is located about 80 kms north of Mexico City, and 1,700 kms from Chichén Itzá.

The Toltec presence in Chichén Itzá is particularly noticeable in the architecture, sculpture, ceramics, paintings and religion. Some examples are: the slope or slant of the foundations of the stone masonry buildings, the colonnades, the reclining idols called "chacmools", the idols named "atlantes", the feathered serpents, depictions of eagles devouring hearts, the ball courts, scenes of human sacrifices found on murals and reliefs, and the ceramics found during excavation, all of which are very typical of this culture.

Some researchers believe that the Toltec art and architecture of the northern sector of Chichén Itzá, as described above, did not originate in Tula, but rather that the governing priest Kukulcán or Quetzalcoatl, left Yucatán and moved to Tula, introducing the new cultural elements there. In other words, they have tried to prove that there was no Toltec influence at Chichén Itzá. They.also say that from A.D. 1185 to 1350, Chichén Itzá saw the construction of such buildings as the Castillo or Temple of Kukulcán, the Temple of the Warriors and the Thousand Columns, the Platform of the Jaguars and Eagles, the Temple of Venus, the Market, the Tzompantli or Skull Rack, and others, which differ in many ways from the buildings in the Central Group, the styles of which are known by the names of "Puuc" and "Chenes".

The great similarities in the art of both these cultures, the Toltec and the Postclassic Maya of Chichén Itzá (according to Thompson, from A.D. 975 to 1200), are undeniable. Aside from those described above, other examples can be given: the Temple of the Warriors at Chichén Itzá is astoundingly similar to the Temple of Venus (or Pyramid of Tlahuizcalpantecuhtli) at Tula; the latter has carved jaguars walking in single file one behind the other, very much like those carved on walls of the Temple of the Jaguars at Chichén Itzá, with the sole exception that the Tula carvings also include coyotes. Murals in the Temple of the Jaguars at Chichén, depict figures of tall people with features quite different from the Maya there is no doubt that they are Toltecs. The four atlantes in "Old Chichen are carbon copies of the ones at Tula; also easily identified on the columns of the Temple of the Warriors and in the many reliefs on the buildings of this northern group, are figures of various foreign-looking people alternating with some that are obviously Mayas. An unending list of other similarities further proves the strong coalescence of these two cultures.

Almost all historical sources agree that towards the end of the 8th century, or at the very latest, the beginning of the 9th, the Toltec culture arose in the central Mexican plateau; the decline and final abandonment of its capital city, Tula, subsequently occurred in A.D. 1156.

Upon careful analysis, we see that when Kukulcán returned to México from Yucatán at the end of the 10th century (according to historians), the architecture, sculpture, ceramics, etc., of the Northern Group at Chichén Itzá, were just beginning, and that Tula had been settled for many years and its most important buildings had already been erected; thus, it would have been impossible for Kukulcán to have transferred his knowledge from Yucatán to México. It should also be remembered that Kukulcán (according to Bishop Landa) originally came from the west and then returned to México. This confirms that he was not a native of Yucatán, but that he came from the high plateau where he had probably been educated. It is, therefore, obvious that he had to have brought his cultural knowledge from México to the Yucatán region.

Another point that further refutes the aforementioned scientists' conclusions is: had the buildings of the Northern Group at Chichén Itzá originally been built in 1185 (as is said), then it would have been impossible for the Mayas to have taken their culture, particularly their architecture, to Tula, that city having been abandoned in 1156.

It is also known that the architecture of Chichén's Northern Group is not replicated, at least not noticeably, anywhere else in the Maya region. The few remains that have been found at other sites, are but pale reflections of a much later period at Chichén Itzá another indication that it was not originally Maya. In addition, it would have been impossible for Maya craftsmen to have sculpted the four atlantes at "Old Chichén" without having known the Toltecs.

We believe that, in part, all this confusion has come about because the origin of the Itzá is unknown to most researchers they believe them to have been the foreigners who conquered Chichén Itzá in fact, however, (as will be seen further on) they were its founders. They left this area, settling in "Chan-Putún" (nowadays Champotón) and then returned 365 years later (having been absent from A.D. 622 to 987).

Perhaps they returned in the company of dissident Toltec intellectuals who abandoned Tula and joined the Itzá at Champotón, as this return coincides with the Postclassic Period at Chichén Itzá (around A.D. 987).

If the dates indicated by historians are true, one cannot then believe that the Mayas influenced the people of Tula. The influence was actually the other way around. As far as we know, not even traces of Maya architecture, either Puuc or Chenes style, have been found in Tula, where they should have existed, at least, in their more important buildings. No reliefs of human figures with Maya features are found, either; conversely, Toltec features abound in the reliefs at Chichén Itzá.

This description and its deductions should convincingly demonstrate that the Mayas did not influence the Toltecs, but the Toltecs the Mayas.

INTELLECTUAL PROGRESS OF THE MAYA

It can be said, without any doubt, that the Maya culture was the most advanced in the American continent, and one of the most remarkable in the world, at that time. This can be appreciated through its difficult and complex system of hieroglyphic writing, in which, so far, 862 distinct characters or glyphs have been identified. They used the zero in their ingenious vigesimal mathematical system of three position numerals, which allowed them to write numbers to infinity. They had four calendars. The first was a ritual calendar called "Tzolkín", which had 13 months of 20 days each, for a total of 260 days. The second was the "haab" or civil calendar, consisting of 18 months of 20 days each, plus 5 extra days, for a total of 365. When this calendar was combined with the Tzolkín, it became the Calendar Round, whereby a date could only be repeated every 52 years; for them, this

Manner in which the false arch was built.

was somewhat like our century. The third calendar was called the Long Count by the chronologists. It was incredibly complicated and after a period of time, the Mayas abbreviated and replaced it with a more simple system called "Period Ending" notations. These last two calendrical systems were only known to and understood by their scientists.

When the Spaniards arrived, the Mayas were still using the "haab" of 365 days, and to record their most important events, they.used another system called the Short Count or Katun Round which is not a calendar as such as it only dates registered into each katun of 19.71 years. The Katun Round has 13 katuns of 19.71 years- 256.23 cycle.

The Mayas used in this system years of 360 day insted 365.

The Mayas had extraordinary knowledge of astronomy they not only found the orbital rotation of the planet Venus, with an error of only 14 seconds, but they even knew its synodical revolution. In their codices, they also drew tables of eclipses and of zodiacal signs.

In A.D. 682, they discovered what was then the most exact calendar in the world, and which differed from the present scientific calendar by only two-ten thousandths of a day.

Their architecture, for beauty and elaborateness, was unrivaled among the pre-Hispanic nations.

The roofs of their buildings are typified by an angular shape wihich has been variously called: the Maya, corbeled, or false arch. The latter name was given because the arch has no keystone as in the Roman arch; instead, the flat stones that form the faces of the arches or vaults, end in a point away from the arch, as can be seen in the drawing below. This type of construction made their chambers very narrow.

They had no metal tools, or draft or pack animales, neither did they use the wheel. The tools or implements they used for building and sculpting were fashioned from hard stone such as jade, jadeite, basalt, diorite, serpentine and flint; examples of these tools can be seen at various museums around the country.

In the vast Maya territory, 23 dialects were spoken. Those furthest removed from the cultural centers had the greatest amount of variance.

RELIGION

The Mayas were an extremely religious nation. At first, religion wa rather simple, but with the passage of time, the priests complicated it mor and more until it finally became polytheistic.

The Popol Vuh, or Sacred Book of the Mayas, tells the story of th creation, by Gucumatz and Tepeu, of the Quiché Maya (of Guatemala), a well as the history of many secondary dieties. They worshipped the su moon and stars. "Yum Chaac", the rain god, was one of their most impor tant; he is featured with a long nose like an elephant's trunk and is frequen ly seen on the facades of their buildings. They had gods for wind, fire, agr culture, war, wisdom, death, etc. They believed the earth was flat and th the heavens were supported by four brothers called "Bacabes"; they believ the firmament was divided into 13 "estates" or classes, and that in ea there was a god that ruled a world. This group of gods was called **Oxl huntikú** they were the gods of good and of light. Below this world, th believed, were nine layers in which lived the gods of fate and darknes those who caused such misfortunes as diseases, plagues, wars, prolong droughts, etc., and these they called **Bolontikú**. They believed that som times, their gods acted with duality, that is, on occasion they could do go and on others could punish fiercely.

The Rain God at the Great Pyramid of Uxmal. Photo by the autor.

To remain in their godsthey' good graces, they frequently celebrat strange and complicated religious rituals and ceremonies; they believed self-sacrifices with prolonged periods of fasting and abstinence, particula

18

of their favorite foods. They frequently practiced bloodletting from different parts of their bodies; they also sacrificed animals and sometimes, people, especially after the arrival of the Toltecs. They also believed in the immortality of the soul.

FOOD

The Mayas were predominantly an agrarian people whose basic crop was corn or maize. This plant provided an enormous variety of dishes, some of which are still great favorites in Yucatecan cooking.

Aside from corn, they cultivated many kinds of beans, lentils, peppers, squashes, tomatoes, sweet potatoes, yams, mandioc, potatoe vines, etc. They also had a large variety of fruits available, such as: the fruit of the "chicle" or gum-tree (zapodilla), the fruit of a cactus air plant called **pitaya**, various types of plums, guava, sugar apple, **zaramuyo** (a pulpy fruit filled with black seeds), **kanisté** (the Maya words for "tree of the yellow sweet potato"). papaya, avocado, and many others.

They ate the meat of deer, rabbit, hare, paca, javalina or wild boar, raccoom, coati, opossum, turtle, monkey, armadillo, lizard and snake. The birds available were: the peninsula pheasant, wild turkey, partridge, quail, chachalaca and various species of doves and pigeons. They raised chickens and turkeys and, along the coastline, ate many kinds of fish.

HISTORY

Sadly, only those portions of history concerning the northern end of the peninsula are known. Our information comes from: the well-known book Relación de las Cosas de Yucatán (Relation of Things in Yucatán), written by the Franciscan Diego de Landa; reports written by another priest, Diego Lopez de Cogolludo; reports from the local town councils and "encomenderos", as well as other persons actively involved in the public life of that time; and lastly, the Book of Chilam Balam, chronicles written by the natives in the Maya tongue and transcribed phonetically into Spanish script.

Without these reports, the history of this great civilization would have been completely lost to us; and, as previously noted, the archeological explorations have, so far, provided only dates and some events in the evolution of this culture and the construction of its buildings. Researchers have had to rely on the already classified styles of ceramics, on architectural styles, on dates found on stelae —stone slabs with relief carvings of human figures on which dates were also carved, given in cycles of 20, 10 and 5 years— and on dates found on lintels and other parts of buildings; more recently, carbon-14 dating has been used; nevertheless, all these tell us little or nothing about the actual history.

The afore mentioned reports tell us that a large group of people under the command of one Holon Chan, appeared in the southeast of the Yucatán Peninsula in A.D. 242, and headed north into the region of the Chenes, today part of the state of Campeche. From there, they migrated east into the present Republic of Honduras, founding many settlements along the way. Holón Chan's successors continued their wanderings and explorations; in A.D. 462, they came upon the lake of Ziyan-Can Bakhalal (today Lake Bacalar). and there established the headquarters of the Chanes tribe.

Shortly thereafter, they discovered the place known today as Chichén Itzá, but did not settle there. It is quite possible that the hospitability of the place and the existence of various natural wells known as "cenotes", caused them to return on October 18, 514, according to correlations of the Maya and European calendars, as done by Goodman, Martínez Hernández and Thompson, all of whom, working independently, came up with the same date; or in the year 254, according to Spinden's correlations. Historians have called the arrival of this group of emigrants the "lesser arrival".

The "greater arrival" refers to the emigration of the Xiu tribe which, contrary to the opinion of some, occurs at practically the same time and place as the migration of the Chanes. Both these tribes belonged to the same ethnic origin, they spoke the same language, they used the same writing, numbering system, architecture, calendar, etc. It so happens that these events practically coincide with the oldest date found in the Puuc region of northern Yucatán (A.D. 475) at Oxkintok, Maxcanú, and the founding of 514); the difference being barely 39 years.

Diego López de Cogolludo, as quoted by the renowned Yucatecan historian, Juan Francisco Molina Solis, wrote that the natives of the Decadent Period informed him that according to tradition, Lakin Chan was the founder of Chichén Itzá, and that this wise priest was also called Zamná or Itzamná; that he had introduced the hieroglyphic writing, the architecture and the calendar; and that he had named a series of places; other reports indicated that he healed the sick and even raised some from the dead.

Because he had two names (Lakin Chan and Itzamná), his people were referred to as either Chanes or Itzá - the latter using the radical of Itzamná. This analysis refutes the hypothesis that the Itzá had been foreigners who had occupied Chichén Itzá at the beginning of the Postclassic or Toltec Period.

After the founding of Chichén Itzá, another group of Chanes founded Ekbalam (which means "black jaguar"), located about 50 km. north of Chichén, in what today is the municipality of Calotmul. Five buildings still exist there, one for each of its founders, with Ekbalam having been the principal chieftan.

Still another Chanes group, headed by four captains, Kinich-Kakmó, Kinich-Kabul, Cit-Ahcoy and Kit-Ahcutz, founded the city of Itzamná (nowadays Izamal), building temples and palaces, the ruins of which still carry the names of their founders. Many years later, the conquistadores used the stones of these buildings to build their own new city, particularly in the impressive Franciscan convent.

Subsequently, another group of Chanes, under the command of captain Zac-Mutul, founded the city of Mutul (today called Motul), located 42 kms from present-day Mérida. Yet another group settled in Ichcansiho, which became the capital of Yucatán. By the time of the final collapse of the Maya culture this city had been renamed T-hó.

It is quite probable that these centers were governed by Chichén Itzá and were part of its taxation network. Perhaps the excessive tax demands of its rulers provoked the rebellion in which Chichén Itzá was attacked and defeated, with its inhabitants being forced to flee westwards in A.D. 622.

After long and arduous peregrinations the Chanes settled in Chan-Putún o Chakan-Putún (today Champotón in Campeche), occupying it after heavy fighting in A.D. 702, according to the **Chumayel Chronicles.** (Molina Solís believed that Chakán was a synonym for Chan, as proved by the fact that the district in which Ichcansihó was located, and where the Chanes settled, was called Chakán.)

When the Chanes arrived in Chan-Putún it was probably called only Putún, and was then renamed as the Putún of the Chanes (Chan-Putún). After having lived there for about 240 years, they returned to Chichén Itzá to look for their ancestors' homes, led by captains Kak-u-pacat and Bil-huh. After a difficult journey, during which they lost their way many times, they settled in a place they called Dzan, which still exists today close to the city of Ticul. Shortly thereafter, a large segment of this group founded Mayapán.

These data refute Bishop Landa's description he mentions Kukulcán as the founder of Mayapán, possibly his information came from uninformed sources. Historically, however, Kukulcán is linked to Mayapán, as a building similar to the one at Chichén Itzá was built there in his memory, and it is possible that he visited Mayapán at a later date.

After a period of progress, strengthening and regrouping at Mayapán, these Chanes went to war against the Motul until they defeated them. It is believed that the Xiu of Uxmal helped the Itzás (Chanes) of Chan-Putún in wreaking their vengeance. The victorious troops then attacked Izamal and defeated it as well. After all foes had been vanquished, they took possession of Chichén Itzá in A.D. 987.

21

Map showing location of Ekbalam, Izamal, Motul and Ichcanzihó; and the route followed by the Itzá from Chichén to Chan-Putún and back.

This narration should clear up the mystery, which has disconcerted so many researchers, of the origin of the Putunes and their relationship to the Itzá; that is, upon returning to Chichén Itzá, the Chanes or Itzá were also referred to as the Putunes, having lived at Putún for 240 years. In addition, during their sojourn in Campeche, some had migrated to Acalán, the Usumacinta river delta, and to adjacent areas, where they became seamen and fishermen.

Upon again occupying Chichén Itzá, the Chanes-Itzá-Putunes added the Toltec technology that would have reached them at about the same time, or a short while later, and quickly became a large and powerful nation. Their consumer and production needs caused their inhabitants to become active traders, both along the coast of the Gulf of Mexico and out into the Caribbean in canoes, and along the magnificent white paved roads that were built during the Classic Period.

Shortly after the return to Chichén Itzá, the Mayas of the northern end of the Yucatán Peninsula, agreed to form a Confederation. The member towns were Chichén Itzá, Uxmal, Mayapán, Izamal and possibly others, with Mayapan being chosen as the headquarters for this Confederation which lasted close to 200 years (from A.D. 1002 to 1182).

Some researchers do not accept the dates relating to the Confederation because they believe that by that time Uxmal had already been abandoned; recent explorations by I.N.A.H. archeologists, however, confirm that Uxmal continued active until the 11th or 12th centuries. This would now fit the time span of the Confederation that brought peace and harmony to this entire Peninsula, as shown by the progress that was made in these areas.

In 1182, differences arose between the chieftans of Chichén Itzá and Mayapán, which led to a terrible civil war in which Chichén Itzá was defeated with the help of Nahua mercenaries brought from Xicalango (in the present state of Tabasco) by the "caciques of the Cocome dynasty of Mayapán. The mercenaries were fierce warriors who used weapons and combat techniques unknown to the natives, for instance, the bow and arrow.

With the defeat of Chichén Itzá, the majority of its inhabitants migrated south, settling in Tayasal, along the shores of Lake Petén Itzá in Guatemala; the remainder scattered in different directions, and all prisoners were subjected to slavery. With this victory, the hegemony of Mayapán was established, and its 245-year dominance resulted in noticeable decadence.

Between approximately 1402 and 1441, practically the whole population of the Peninsula rebelled against Mayapán and its tyrannical rule of abuses, injustices and heavy taxation.

After bloody battles with ups and downs on both sides, Mayapán was finally defeated and destroyed; all the "caciques" were executed, except for two that had been absent.

At the end of the war, Tutul-Xiu (a descendant of the nobles of Uxmal), who had hoisted the flag of this rebellion, freed the "caciques" of the different districts that had helped in the defeat of Mayapán, allowing each to set the limits of his own territory and to govern as best he could.

When the Spaniards arrived in the mid-16th century, they found the Peninsula divided into 19 districts, each governed by a cacique. Most of them were not on friendly terms with each other and confrontations were constant. They lived an almost primitive life, as in the days of the Formative Period, and this situation certainly helped the foreigners in their conquest.

Some archeologists contend that Chichén Itzá, like other ceremonial centers, was not totally abandoned but continued to be inhabited by some of the descendants of the Postclassic Period and the temples continued to be used; however, the state of ruin in which the Spaniards found the buildings would indicate the opposite. Tradition has it that the Mayas of the Decadent Period were afraid to go near their ancestors' ceremonial centers at night because they believed that, that was when they were visited by the souls of their forefathers.

What is positively known, is that the Sacred Cenote continued to be visited and used for ceremonies and sacrifices by pilgrims from many areas who subsequently returned to their homes, and that the ceramics found at the Cenote were brought by these pilgrims at these different times.

Quite possibly, upon abandoning Chichén Itzá, some of the inhabitants settled in the neighboring village of Pisté, two miles west. There is an important cenote there called Cunanchén with crystalline, drinkable water. This resettlement is confirmed by Molina Solis who writes: "At the time that Captain Francisco de Montejo arrived in Chichén Itzá, he particularly noticed the ruins of the great buildings, remains of an ancient grandeur, like a metropolis of the Itzá. Near the ruins was an Indian village governed by Nacón Cupul." It is almost certain that this village refers to the one we know today as Pisté. It is also very possible that the villagers of Pisté went to Chichén Itzá from time time to clear the undergrowth from around the buildngs, hoping to delay their destruction by vegetation. Perhaps that is why the buildings known as the Iglesia or Church, the Temple of the Nuns and the Red House where less ruined than others at the time of the conquest.

CHICHEN ITZA

This name is formed by three Maya words: chi meaning mouth, chen meaning well, and Itzá being the name of the tribe that settled there; thus, "the mouth of the well of the Itzá's". This was probably not the name it had at the height of its splendour; in fact, it is almost certain that the Mayas renamed it during the Decadent Period. One would suppose that if a stranger at that time had asked the name of the place, they would hardly have answered: "This is the mouth of the well of the Itzá." Why would they have spoken in the third person, as if talking of someone else, when referring to themselves?

Eric S. Thompson, in his book **Maya History and Religion** quotes Ralph Roys as saying that the original name for Chichén Itzá could have been **Uuc-hab-nal**; yet in his work entitled **The Rise and Fall of the Maya Civilization**, he gives the name as **Uucyabnal** which translates into "the Seven Great Properties". It is not known if this change was due to carelessness in writing, or a printing error or the result of subsequent research, since **Uuc-hab-nal** means, uuc seven, **hab** year, and **nal** corn, or "the seven years of corn , perhaps referring to seven years of plentiful corn harvests in that area. Other Mayaists translate Itzá as: **itz** sorcerer, in the Cakchiquel Maya dialect, spoken in the central region, and **há** water, which would have meant "the mouth of the well of the Water Sorcerer".

We must remember, however, that the Cakchiquel dialect does not belong to this region, and its usage here is inappropriate, particularly because it is known that in the Yucatecan Maya dialect, the words uay, **sayan, ts'utan** and **ah pul yah** mean sorcerer or wizard. Besides, when the Spaniards arrived, the Sacred Cenote was called Chen-Kú; chen meaning well and **kú** god, or "the well of God"; thus, it could not have been the well of the sorcerer, a sorcerer being the opposite of God.

We do know that the word Itzá is still used as a surname and that since ancient times, the Mayas have used the names of plants and animals and different expressions as patronymics, without their meanings necessarily having any relationship with the person so named.

Chichén Itzá covers an area of approximately 3 kms from north to south and 1.5 kms from east to west. It is divided into three sectors: The Central Group, the oldest and the one corresponding to the Classic and Postclassic Periods; the Southern Group, also pertaining to these two periods, with the name "Old Chichén having been given by Edward Herbert Thompson; and the Northern Group, the most recent and pertaining to the Postclassic or Toltec Period. This leads us to believe that the Toltecs, upon arrival,

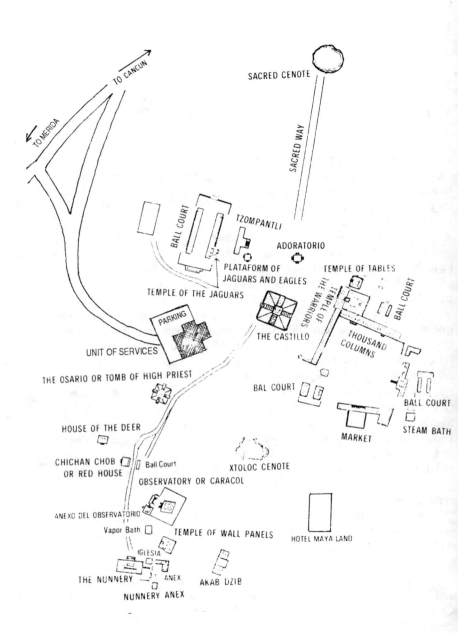

Map of Chichén Itzá

joined the Mayas in the Central Group, and then both cultures together planned the Northern Group.

It has been said that the archeological sites of the Maya territory, such as Chichén Itzá, Uxmal, Kabah, Copán, etc., were not cities but ceremonial centers. Some of the buildings were palaces where the nobility lived, others were temples and yet others administrative buildings; the rest consisted of markets, schools, observatories, etc. Craftsmen and peasants lived in the surrounding areas in straw-thatched huts of varying sizes and types according to their economic statu-s; they had access to the ceremonial centers when a religious or profane rite was being held, on market days and when they had important matters to resolve or negotiate.

It is also known, by remains found in some of the buildings, that almost all these buildings were painted in bright colors both inside and out.

The colors used by the ancient Mayas were both vegetable and mineral in origin. Among the former, indigo is mentioned as producing blue; red was produced by the "achiote" bush (Bixa orellana L.) with capsule-shaped fruit enclosing many small seads (these seads are still used today as seasoning for stews) and another tree known as "palo de tinte" or "palo Campeche" (Hematoxylon campechianum L.). The bark and the wood of the mulberry tree produced a brownish yellow and also green. Charcoal, finely ground and processed, produced black. Another herbaceous plant of this region, which the natives called choch quitam (javalina intestines). produced yellow from its boiled roots.

The red earth found in some parts of this region, produced vermilion, and lime produced white.

Once they had their primary colors, they mixed these to produce other shades, making them lighter or darker, as is done today with manufactured pigments.

There is no doubt that in preparing their paints, the Mayas used ingredients which are unknown to us and which have allowed the paint to resist the ravages of time.

DESCRIPTION OF THE NORTHERN GROUP

(All these buildings have Toltec influence.)

We now know that the Yucatán Peninsula has been inhabited since 8000 B.C. or earlier. Evidence of human habitation was found at Chichén Itzá dating back to 2000 B.C.; however, they were probably semi-migratory groups of people that did not evolve culturally, nor did they have any connection with the founders and builders of this important ceremonial center, who seem to have arrived already possessing an advanced culture.

The original names and actual uses that the ancient Mayas gave their buildings is unknown. By the time the Spanish conquistadores arrived, these centers had been abandoned for many decades and for the most part, the monuments were in very poor condition, mainly due to the dense vegetation that had overrun the sites, and the inclement weather.

The names we use today to identify the buildings were given, for one reason or another, either by the Spaniards or the archeologists.

THE CASTILLO OR TEMPLE OF KUKULCAN

Captain Francisco de Montejo, the Spanish and his retinue, named this great pyramid the "Castillo", when they first saw it in 1527.

At the time of the conquest, the Franciscan Diego de Landa, was told by the natives that this pyramid was built in honor of Kukulcán, a bearded man that arrived in the Yucatán Peninsula during the latter part of the 10th century, accompanied by a large group of followers, and who wore a full-length tunic and sandals. It was said that he came from the southwest and preached the need to build idols of stone, pottery and wood; that he forced people to worship these, and to offer sacrifices of plants, animals, human blood and even human hearts; and that he suggested that a pyramid be built in his memory. Because of these reports, which coincide with the carving of a bearded man on the western door jamb of the main entrance, this pyramid was named "The Temple of Kukulcán".

This structure consists of nine superimposed platforms, each. platform being somewhat smaller than the one below. The summit is topped by a building with a wide entrance in front (north side), giving access to a narrow, rectangular chamber, 11.15 meters long; the roof is supported by two

El Castillo or Temple of Kukulcan as it looked in 1842 according to this Catherwood print.

The Castillo or Temple of Kukulcán, as restoration began, (note the steel scaffolding). Photo by A. Cabrera, courtesy of Irma Cantón de Cárdenas.

The Castillo or temple of Kukulkán, after restoration. Photo by José López Nájera.

The Castillo or temple of Kukulkán during light and shadow phenomenon on equinoctial days. Photo by José López Nájera.

cylindrical columns, each carved in the shape of a serpent's body. At the back of this chamber, a door leads to another smaller one, supported by walls and two square columns in the center that held up the roof, these still have the original wooden, relief-carved lintels, although parts are missing stolen by vandals chopping at them with machetes. On the west, south and east sides, other doors connect to a narrow, U-shaped chamber.

Restoration has been completed on the western and northern sections and parts of the eastern section; the remainder has recently been braced. The pyramid's dimensions are the following: the base is 55.30 meters long on each side; it is 30 meters high, with 24 meters accounting for the body of the pyramid and 6 meters for the temple; its stairways are 8.85 meters wide, with 91 steps in each, plus one step more which is not included because it is part of the platform. Due to a series of coincidences, it has been assumed that this pyramid represents the Maya civil calendar in which each side represents one of the seasons of the year and the steps the days of the year. Each side has 91 steps, multiplied by four, equals 364, plus the platform step, thus giving the 365 days of the year.

Looking at only one face of the pyramid, we can see that there are nine corners on each side formed by the superimposed platforms, adding both sides, we get 18, which were the months of their year. Each month has 20 days; 18 times 20 equals 360, plus one "ill-fated" month of 5 days, for a grand total of 365 days - the Vague Year calendar. The 52 sunken panels found on the pyramid are said to represent the number of years in the Maya life cycle.

Some years ago, the archeological site's clean-up crews noticed that on the equinoctial days (March 21 and September 22) at sunset, between 5:00 and 5:30 p.m., the shadows made by the northwest corners of the platforms, were successively cast along the edge of the northern stairway, from the top downwards, until the play of light and shadow created what appeared to be the body of an enormous serpent descending the pyramid; the last shadowy ondulation stops at the neck of the huge, stone reptile's head that rests on the ground at the base of the stairs.

Lic. Luis Arochi, a member of the Astronomy Society of Mexico and the American Society on Anthropology, has popularized this phenomenon of light and shadow to the point where many thousands of people each year now come to see this magnificent show. In his research, Arochi also discovered that during the winter solstice (December 22), if one stands on the southwest side of the Ball Court's platform at sunrise, one can see the sun ascend along the edge of the northern stairway to the temple and then continue on its course, giving the impression that the sun climbs up the stairway.

THE BURIED TEMPLE

According to custom, the Maya, like other Mesoamerican cultures, covered or buried their temples by using the older structures as foundations for the newer, higher ones. Some, of course, immediately suggested that the Mayas buried their buildings every 52 years, which in their Calendar Round system was the end of a cycle; logic, however, would indicate otherwise. For instance, at Uxmal, the Pyramid of the Magician has five substructures, and according to carbon-14 dating of the wooden lintels, the first substructure dates back to A.D. 569; more recent studies have shown that this site was abandoned during the 12th century, which would thus have equalled 11 periods of 52 years; had that theory been valid, this building would have had 11 substructures. Here at Chichén Itzá, in this Northern Group, only the Castillo and the Temple of the Warriors have substructures; it is believed that these buildings were in use from approximately A.D. 975 to 1196, which is equal to four periods of 52 years we therefore believe this theory can now safely be ruled out.

In 1931, archeologists with the I.N.A.H., started excavating on the south side of the Castillo or Temple of Kukulcán and tunneled towards the center, to check if this structure actually rested on another; they found it had, indeed, been built over a smaller temple. On not finding a stairway on that side, or on the western side, they dug another tunnel under the northern stairway, running west to east, and built an angular roof like the Maya architects had used. Upon reaching the halfway mark of the outside stairway, they tunneled to the right, toward the center of the buried temple, where they found four wide staircases leading downwards. At the bottom of the stairs was a stone box; they removed the cover, and found it contained human bones, two flint daggers, a beautiful necklace of various sizes of jade beads, a jade pendant with a relief carving of a seated figure, and two turquoise mosaics. The jade objects and the flint daggers are now at the Archeological Museum of Mérida, and the turquoise mosaics are at the México City Museum of Anthropology; the bones have disappeared. The stone chest or box, with its cover, is still at the entrance to the tunnel.

The archeologists continued excavating upwards, and after 62 steps, reached the upper platform on which the Maya-Toltecs had built two rectangular chambers. In the first chamber, they found a reclining idol of the type called "chacmool", with eyes and nails made of seashells one of the best-preserved of the 13 chacmools found. In the second chamber, in back, they found a block of masonry inside of which was a magnificent jaguar, sculpted from a solid block of stone; it was painted red, its eyes were of jade and its teeth of flint. It is believed that this jade came from Asia (possibly China); the other 72 pieces of jade, which simulate the jaguar's spots, are probably from Guatemala, where jade mines have been discov-

ered. On the animal.s flat back there is a round mosaic set with turquoises, now protected by a glass cover. The jaguar was carved in profile, with its head turned forward and a fierce expression on its face. It is now a familiar sight its photograph has been published in many magazines and books on archeology and on post cards.

Red Jaguar. Photo Courtesy of Luis Ramírez Aznar

The façade of this temple consists of jaguars embedded or set into the wall, and as complementary ornamentation, it has reliefs of interwined serpents and rosettes with fringes hanging from them.

TEMPLE OF THE JAGUARS

About 160 meters northwest of the Castillo, and forming part of the side of the Ball Court, is the building known as the Temple of the Jaguars. The lower portion, facing east, consists of a raised platform, about 12 meters high, on which rests a rectangular building. It was named the Temple of the Jaguars because around its perimeter are carvings of 32 of these felines, marching in twos and separated by circles with fringes hanging from them. These circles enclose heartshaped reliefs, which some have interpreted as grains of corn and others as serpents rattles. Long, feathered serpents ornament the back of this building. Some of the colors originally used on this building (particularly the reds and blues) can still be seen.

In this raised platform is a rectangular chamber, the roof of which is supported by walls and at the entrance, by two rectangular columns. Between these columns is a jaguar, sculpted from a solid block of stone, and similar in both type and size, to the red jaguar found in the Castillo s substructure.

The most beautiful carvings of all Chichén Itzá are found in this chamber five rows of warriors parading from the ends of the chamber towards the center, one row on top of the other, covering the whole interior. These

34

Temple of Jaguars, as restoration was starting. Photo by A. Cabrera, courtesy of Irma Cantón de Cárdenas.

Temple of the Jaguars, after the restoration was completed. Photo by the autor.

rows of warriors are separated by intertwined serpents going in opposite directions around the perimeter of the chamber, with one head and one tail at each end. The warriors are richly dressed and on some, the colors of the paint can still be seen. The proportions of the figures the fine details, reveal the high level of craftsmanship attained by these artists of yesteryear. On some of the warriors, one can still see the wrinkles on their faces, and their fingernails, as well as the weave of the cloth and its decorations. Quite a few are bearded, and it is believed that the one in the center represents Kukulcán-Quetzalcoatl, mentioned by Bishop Landa in his well known **Relation.**

On the columns supporting the roof of this building, archeologist Manuel Cirerol Sansores found reliefs that he interpreted as an allegory on the origin of the world animal life, plant life, human beings and death. Each column is divided into three parts and the contents are the same on all four sides. First, at the bottom, is an impressive face which. according to Cirerol, represents the Creator; tears stream from His eyes, spreading in all directions, forming the waters of the world; also, from these tears, plants sprout, representing the earth's vegetation; and from there, emerge the fish and molluscs that inhabit the waters. Then the amphibious turtle appears, and immediately the swan that walks, swims and flies. After creating all these creatures, the Creator believed it was necessary to have a more perfect being that would understand and love Him man. From His brain emerges the serpent and then the human, occupying the central portion of the column, with the reptile wound around his body. Perhaps that is why the Mayas use the serpent as the symbol of life and fertility.

The opposite column (on the north side). depicts in relief a woman in a long skirt decorated with crossed bones; her face is a skull, symbolizing death. This pictogram tells us that all that has life ends in death. Cirerol named these columns the Cosmogonics.

The upper level (facing west) of the Temple of the Jaguars, a sort of an annex to the Ball Court, has a wide entrance in front supported by two

Church and Observatory showing how the maya buildins are inclined. Photo by the autor.

Detail of cosmogonic columns, showing origin of the world and of life.
Photo courtesy of Javier Medina Riancho.

Mural in the Temple of the Jaguars. Oficial Guide book by the I.N.A.H

Part of cosmogonic columns, showing origin of the world and of life. Photo courtesy of Javier Medina Riancho.

thick, cylindrical columns carved to represent the bodies of two enormous feathered serpents, the heads of which rest on the floor; each head is fashioned from a single block of stone, and weighs about six tons; the serpents' tails form part of the capital of each column, with the rattles pointing upwards, at right angles.

How these enormous heads were transported up there continues to be a mystery, although it is assumed that ramps and rollers were used.

Each of the chambers in this building is 11 meters long and 7 meters high. The lintel over the door of the inside chamber is of sapodilla wood (Achras sapota L.). which is so hard that it is even difficult to cut and carve with today's metal tools. The work of these ancient builders is truly incredible, considering they carved such fine work with only the most basic of stone tools. The second chamber used to be covered with beautifully painted murals, some portions of which can still be seen.

One section of the west wall depicts the scene of a rather disorderly village of straw- or palmthatched huts, very much like the ones still being built and used by the Maya peasants of today; women are shown going about their household chores. The lower portion of this same mural, depicts marching warriors dressed in short skirts; each is holding various lances in the right hand and a shield in the left.

Although some believe this scene is a battle, it appears to be more of a practice or training session, or possibly, a ceremony .in honor of the war god, because the lances carried by these warriors are pointed either upwards or downwards, but not at each other; nor can one see lance-pierced or wounded warriors lying about. On the same wall there is a colored painting of a canoe and a strawthatched hut.

On the wall opposite the warriors, one can see two figures of very tall people; there is no doubt that they represent Toltecs.

37

The Ball Court as Catherwood saw it. Then so called "Sacred Podium" in the back grownd.

Ball Court, prior to restoration (after vegetation had been cleared). Photo by A. Cabrera, courtesy of Irma Cantón de Cárdenas.

Ball Court, after restaroation was completed. Photo by the Autor.

On the southwest side, very steep steps were built to reach these chambers, although they could also be reached by long, unrestored stairways located on either side of the back of these lateral walls.

THE BALL COURT

The ritual ball game was practiced by many Mesoamerican cultures including some primitive tribes in Arizona (U.S.A.), where an enormous ball court was found similar to the ones in Mexico, but with crudely fashioned walls in which stone rings had been set.

In Mesoamerica, even though the courts are similar, each has its own special characteristics, which would indicate that the ritual ball game was not practiced in exactly the same manner, but rather that each region had its own rules.

The ball court at Chichén Itzá was thought to have been the most important one; but not long ago, another, even larger, was found at Tula; however, it has not yet been restored.

Unfortunately, the name of the game and the manner in which it was practiced are unknown. By the time the Spanish conquistadores arrived, the place had been abandoned for more than 300 years, and the main ball court, along with four other smaller ones, scattered throughout this site, had been quite destroyed and covered by the dense vegetation.

The reliefs show seven players facing in one direction and seven facing in the other, so that they are, in effect, facing each other. The uniforms of these players consist of a short skirt and a wide belt in which is tucked what appears to be a small bat; the headdress sported a long crest of feathers (some are shown carrying the headdress on their back). From the shoulders to the wrists they wear protective padding; they also have protective pad-

Ball player in full uniform.
Photo by the Autor.

Ball players. Captain on the left with a knife in his right hand and a human head in his left; oppoosite him on the right, the headless, kneeling captain of the other team. Photo: Indian Art of México and Central América by Miguel Covarrubias, page 288.

Catherwood drawings, showing the reliefs of one of the two Ball Court rings.

Ball player. Photo by the Autor

ding on one knee, on the hip and on the left ankle; each player holds a serpent-shaped object in his right hand. The two captains are at the center; one of them holds a flint knife in one hand, and in the other, a human head from which blood is pouring, symbolized by corn leaves. The captain of one team is headless and kneeling; seven spurts of blood shoot from his neck, these change into serpents, except for one, which sprouts a long vine covered in flowers and fruit. As there are six remaining players and six spurts of blood, it has been assumed that the captain was sacrificed on behalf of all the members of his team, and that his blood was a symbolic fertilizer in hopes of better harvests.

Between the two captains, is a skull enclosed in a circle; a bifurcate scroll projects from its mouth, symbolizing words.

Some believe that it is the winning captain who cuts off the head of the looser; others believe the opposite is true, that the winner is the one sacrificed, because of the honor of giving up one's life to the gods. We should keep in mind, however, that the will to survive is strong in humans, and the mere thought that as winner one was going to lose one's head at the end of the game with one swift stroke, would probably be enough to forego that honor. It may also be possible that this sacrifice was only simulated.

The structure at the south end of the court was named "the Theater", speculation being that the nobles sat there to watch the game which, aside from being sport. and entertainment, was also a ceremony dedicated to the god of agriculture, as indicated by these reliefs.

On the north end, opposite the Theater and at a distance of 170 meters, is another smaller, higher building known today as "the Sacred Dais". It is believed that the king sat there with his entourage of priests to watch the game. Possibly, people with certain social status were also allowed to watch, sitting or standing along the platforms formed by the tops of the lateral walls; this has been assumed because along the back of these walls are long stairways, now in ruins. It is believed that workers and peasants were not allowed to watch, much less participate in, these events which were only for the privileged classes.

The Ball Court, between the two walls, is 40 meters wide; the lateral walls are 12 meters high. Close to the upper edge and in the center of each wall, a stone ring is embedded in the rock, through which a rubber ball was passed. Each end of the court is an open-ended T. Conjectures about how this game was played are many. Some researchers claim that the players did not use their hands, only their shoulders, elbows, one hip, the right knee and the left ankle. Without the use of hands, it seems impossible that the ball could have been passed through this relatively small ring set at such a great height. Should someone try it today, it is almost certain that it could not be done. If, in fact, they did not use their hands, what then would be the purpose of the flat object in the right hand or the bat tucked

41

into the belt?

The most astonishing features of this Ball Court are its echo and acoustics. If you stand on the Sacred Dais and someone else stands just inside the Theater, you can easily carry on a conversation in a normal tone of voice. If you fling a coin on to something solid, you can hear it ring across the field. If you stand under either of the two rings and make a short, sharp sound, or clap your hands once, the echo will repeat at least twelve times, provided there is no other noise or a strong wind.

On top of the lateral platforms, it is still possible to see the remains of three small buildings on the west wall and of two on the east wall; perhaps the judges sat there to referee the games.

THE TZOMPANTLI OR SKULLL RACK

Next to the Platform of the Jaguars and Eagles, is a T shaped platform. The cross bar of the T has the sides completely covered with skulls carved in relief, apparently attached by a vertical stake in rows of four. The Aztecs used to skewer the heads of their prisoners of war like trophies to such stakes (particularly those of high military rank); because of this similarity, this platform was named Tzompantli, a word of Nahua origin. The vertical portion of the T has interesting reliefs of people, some holding sharp lances in their hands, feathered and scaled serpents, eagles, and other motifs.

The dimensions of this platform are: the top of the T, running north-south, is 60 meters long and 15 meters wide; the vertical portion of the T is 14 meters long and 2 meters high. At the base of the T, facing east, are the only access steps to the top of the platform. When it was excavated in 1940, no human bones or urns with ashes were found; this might have supported the contention of some, that it had been used as a burial site for important officials. From inside the platform, however, a stone ring was unearthed, similar to the ones used in ball games, but without the bracket piece that would have shown it had been embedded in a wall. Also discovered inside, was a chacmool (number 13), characterized by its unique form and expression.

The late Yucatecan archeologist, Manuel Cirerol Sansores, believed that this structure could have been a memorial to the soldiers that lost their lives defending their homeland; the letter "T" symbolizes the wind and the vertical ribbons joining the skulls and painted blue (heaven being blue) seemed to point to the souls of these brave soldiers floating in space.

Adoratorio or Platform of Venus. Photo by José López Nájera.

THE PLATFORM OF THE JAGUARS AND EAGLES

About 3 meters from the Skull Rack, is a small platform with stairs on all four sides. At one time, it had been named, erroneously, the Platform of the Tigers and Eagles; but, of course, there have never been tigers in the Americas, only jaguars. At each corner there is an exquisitely carved jaguar sitting on its haunches, and facing an eagle; both are holding a heart in their claws, as if to devour it. Issueing from the mouth of the jaguar and the beak of the eagle are scrolls, symbolizing spoken words, and insinuating that the animals are holding a conversation. Because there are no eagles in Yucatán, and because animals of different species cannot communicate with each other, the author of this book believes that the eagle symbolizes an important Toltec official who came to make arrangements with his Maya colleague (the jaguar) on instituting human sacrifices at Chichén Itzá.

Along the cornice of this platform, are reliefs of seated figures, leaning slightly backwards; each is holding a very elaborate lance. These figures are very similar to the ones that decorate the superimposed platforms of the Temple of the Warriors.

ADORATORIO OR TEMPLE OF VENUS

This is a square platform located about 100 meters north of the Castillo. Its sides are 18 meters long and 4 meters high, with stairs on all four sides. This structure was so named because it has eight stars, incompletely carved, two in each corner, which archeologists have interpreted as representing the planet Venus. On the corners and stairs are figures of monsters with mammal's shoulders and arms and claws of a bird; a human face emerges from the open mouth with forked tongue. The upper portion, in the shape of a crest, is adorned with long feathers which some believe to be corn leaves. Beautifully sculpted along the cornice of this platform are the bodies of ondulating serpents with long feathers that had been painted green, and between each ondulation are tadpoles, possibly symbolizing the phenomenon of metamorphosis. Some of the original colors can still be seen on these reliefs today.

Over the years, this platform has received many other names as well: Platform of the Dance, of the Rites of Fire, and of the Cones; the latter, because along its edges are various cones fashioned in calcareous stone, each of which, if tapped with something solid, emits a different tonal sound. It was also called the Platform of the Pineapples because some reliefs close to the stairs seem to look like this fruit; actually, these are components of the hieroglyph **Pop**, the first month of the Maya calendar.

A little more than a century ago, a foreigner named Augustus Leplongeon came to Yucatán looking for archeological treasure; at that time, the enormous value of Chichén Itzá was practically unknown, and it was easy for visitors to do as they pleased. Leplongeon, with total impunity, proceeded to blow up this platform with charges of gunpowder, possibly to save time or labor, but thereby destroying part of the its sculpted stonework. He did find, however, the first reclining idol, which he named "chacmool", believing it to represent a jaguar knight. This particular chacmool has been in Mexico City's Museum of Anthropology for a number of years.

Subsequently, other reclining idols were found, at Tula as well as in other centers that had had Toltec influence, and these, too, were given the name chacmool. When the Spaniards built the Chichén Itzá "hacienda", they used some of the carved stones from this platform to build the water troughs for their corrals.

Another idol was later found in this platform; the figure was almost life-size, seated and naked, with its elbows resting on its knees, and the righ: leg and foot twisted inwards as if deformed; perhaps it represented an important deity of that time. Today, it can be seen at the Museum of Archeology in Mérida.

THE SACRED CENOTE OR WELL OF SACRIFICE

About 350 meters north of the Gastillo, is the Sacred Cenote. The word "cenote", used in designating these enormous natural wells, was originally the Maya word **dsonote** which the Spaniards changed to "tzonote" because they could not pronounce it; this.later became cenote, and was incorporated into the Spanish language.

Cenotes are geological formations occurring in the Yucatán Peninsula, particularly in limestone areas. Generally, these cenotes are caves with stalactites hanging from the roofs; others, like this one, are open, water-filled wells with almost vertical walls. The depth of the water table varies in accordance with the well's distance from the sea: the closer it is to the coast, the closer the water table is to the surface. For instance, if a well is drilled at 200 or 300 meters from the beach, the water table is at a depth of about 2 meters; at 35 kms, the depth is about 8 meters; and at 160 kms, the water table is at a depth of almost 40 meters. The water also becomes purer the further inland it is from the coast. These natural formations or cenotes, as well as the artificial wells are interconnected by underground streams which are assumed to be filtrations from the sea, losing their salinity as they travel through the soil.

In the center of this archeological region, there are two cenotes of practically the same size: one was named "Sacred" or "of Sacrifice", which when the Spaniards arrived, the Mayas had been calling **Chen-kú**, signifying "well of God". The other was called **Xtoloc**, and it shall be described separately.

There are more than 15 cenotes in the surrounding countryside, at distances varying from 1 to 7 kilometers from this site.

Over the years, many archeologists have measured this Cenote of Sacrifice. The last set of measurements were taken in 1967, and are as follows: it is slightly oval-shaped, its north-south diameter is 59 meters and its east-west diameter is 60.5 meters; the water stands 22 meters below ground level; the bottom of the well is funnelshaped and at its center is 20 meters deep, 13.4 meters are actually water and the remainder is mud. It has been calculated as having 23.000 cubic meters of water, and its temperature varies from 20. to 23.C.

This cenote was first explored by Edward Herbert Thompson, an amateur archeologist (not to be confused with Eric S. Thompson, the reknowned British archeologist). Thompson arrived in Yucatán in 1895, as the United States Vice Oonsul; he already had some knowledge of the history of this area and had heard of the human sacrifices. Tradition has it that the Mayas threw their most beautiful young virgins, dressed in their best clothes and jewelry, into this enormous well, there to drown as offerings to **Yum chaac** (the rain god), whenever their crops were failing because of lack of rain.

To be able to explore this area properly, Thompson purchased the Chi

Sacred Cenote. Photo by the Autor.

chén Itzá "hacienda", which the Spanish conquistadores had built with the stones of the ruined buildings. He thereupon brought diving equipment in and hired two young Greek sponge divers.

Exploration work was carried out between 1903 and 1907; other historians record the dates as between 1904 and 1911. Thompson only briefly described the objects he found in the Sacred Cenote; perhaps for fear that he would be told to return them or that he would have to pay a large indemnity, which ultimately did occur. Through other sources, it became known that among the numerous and varied objects he found, are following: a) a large collection of carved pieces of jade, including beads for necklaces (some broken, some whole); b) gold objects such as rings, small bells, sandals, candlesticks, tiaras or diadems, figurines, embossed laminas, and others; c) copper chisels, bells and other objects; d) handles of fans, pyrite mirrors, sacrificial knives with gold handles, points of lances, fragments of staffs of command, wooden dolls decorated with rubber and copal, numerous figurines, various pottery artifacts and 43 incomplete human skeletons, of which 14 have been identified as male, 21 as belonging to children from 18 months to 12 years of age, and 8 being females (ages 7 to 21). These findings contradict the story of young virgins having been the principal sacrifices; obviously, preference was given to children. As to the adult skeletons, historian Molina Solis says that during the Decadent Period, criminals were taken to Chichén Itzá and thrown into the Cenote as punishment.

Of the jewelry and valuable objects found, some were sent to the Peabody Museum in Cambridge, Massachusetts, and some to the Field Museum in Chicago, Illinois. In 1976, at the request of the Mexican government, part of this collection was returned. The jade pieces can now be seen at the Archeology Museum in Mérida.

Unfortunately for archeology, these explorations were carried out in a very disorganized manner, in relation to the stratigraphy of the bottom of the well or the different layers that would have marked the periods in which these artifacts were thrown into the great well. Among the jade pieces, two carried dates: one date is equivalent to A.D. 690, and is believed to have come from Palenque; the other date is equivalent to A.D. 706, and comes from Piedras Negras, Guatemala. It is not known if they had been ancient relics.

In 1935. the Yucatecan archeologist Manuel Cirerol Sansores, at that time head of the archeological area of Yucatán, requested that he be allowed to drag or dewater the well using powerful pumps; permission was denied.

In view of this denial, and believing that Thompson might have missed some things in the mud that had been brought up, he proceeded to sift through it again with the help of some Maya workers. He found a small, but significant, collection of gold, jade, flint and pottery objects, the most outstanding of which was a beautifully carved gold frog with turquoise

Part of the equipment used in the 1967-68 explorations of the Sacred Cenote. Photo courtesy of Luis Ramírez Aznar.

eyes; the skills of that ancient goldsmith easily rivals any of today's craftsmen. The frog is now on display at the Archeology Museum in Mérida.

The second major exploration of this cenote, took place in late 1960 and early 1961, under the direction of the I.N.A.H., and with the technical cooperation of the Mexican Aquatic Sports and Explorations Club (C.E.D.A.M.). This work was also partially financed, in addition to the above two, by the National Geographic Society and the Insight Company, in the United States, in exchange for the right to film a television documentary.

In his Preliminary Report, the well-known writer and archeologist, Roman Piña Chan, gives a wealth of detail on the procedures followed during the 1960-61 explorations, as well as those carried out in 1967-68, having actively participated in both as one of the principal directors. In the earlier one, he mentions the collaboration of an able group of people, among them, Pablo Bush Romero, Norman Scott, Ponciano Salazar, William J. Folan, Jr., and Raúl Pavón; in the later exploration, he also mentions archeologist Victor Segovia Pinto, who was trained as a diver, as well as 40 other technicians, each specializing in a different activity.

Piña Chan writes that in the 1960-61 exploration, an "air-lift" was used. This is a type of compressed air suction pump that sucks up water, plus the mud and sediment from the bottom, through a 10" aluminum pipe. The contents were pumped into a raft where the mud was sifted and objects of archeological interest were removed. This operation was subsequently stopped because the fragile pieces broke too easily.

During this exploration, studies and sketches of the configuration of the bottom of the well were made; it also produced various gold, silver and copper bells; a copper disk with the image of Tlaloc; a pendant shaped like a turtle with bells; various jade beads and engraved plaques; a stone knife with a wooden handle covered in gold leaf; wood figurines, copal incense balls, bits of cloth, copper rings; wooden ear discs set with bits of jade and turquoise; small, three-legged, copal-decorated plates, and other objects, that were taken to the I.N.A.H. laboratories to be cleaned and studied.

The last exploration promoted by C.E.D.A.M. was carried out in 1967-68, with the assistance of Norman Scott. The original project involved the pumping and clarifying of water by means of a modified and controlled "air-lift"; however, a "hydro-lift" project was finally accepted and approved.

Work started in mid-September, 1967, and ended in April, 1968, at a cost of six million pesos. Scott undertook to arrange the financing; this was obtained from Expeditions Unlimited, Inc., and other private industry enterprises and publishing firms in the U.S., as well as contributions by I.N.A.H., C.E.D.A.M. and the Mexican national oil company, PEMEX.

The following equipment was brought in: two electrical power plants with a pumping capability of 36,000 liters of water per hour; a telescopic hoist; a square platform, 15 meters long on each side, used as a raft and capable of supporting a weight of 50 tons; portable buildings, trailers and other necessary equipment. The water was pumped into a nearby depression. After a few days of pumping, the water had dropped to three meters below its natural level and there it remained almost stationary, going down only about an inch with constant pumping; the underground filtrations were replacing the water as fast as it could be pumped out, so the pumping operation was halted.

The bottom was explored for a short while, and a few objects of archeological value were found. Subsequently, the water was clarified by chemical substances until it turned blue and transparent, allowing visibility to depths of 8 to 10 meters. This was a help to the divers who had had some health problems due to murky water.

These explorations resulted in findings of portions of wooden buckets, fragments of ropes and cords, bits of charred cloth, copal incense balls; small, three-legged plates painted blue, jade beads; numerous human long bones, vertebrae and skulls; copper bells and rings (some rings were of filigree or wire), various pieces of ceramics (some whole, some in shards); two beautifully carved wooden stools, one in the shape of a turtle, the other with a portion jutting out in the shape of a serpent's head, similar to those found in the high plateau of Mexico; small wooden masks, gold and copper sandals, gold bells, small jade plaques, rubber balls and bits of rubber. The majority of the ceramics were of the Puuc era.

Piña Chan, who describes all these findings, believes that because of the sacrificial knives that were found, the victims' hearts were cut out prior to their weighted-down bodies being thrown into the well. He also believes that the wooden stools were used by those waiting to be sacrificed.

On the south bank of the cenote, the ancient Mayas built three small masonry chambers at different levels. It is believed that the two western chambers were used as steam baths or "temazcal" for the purification of the victims. The eastern chamber consists of two floors, one above the other, with a round hole between them. The lower area is round and access is through a small rectangular entrance. It is speculated that the victims were placed in the upper portion and perfumed with copal incense so that the evil spirits would not interfere with their journey to the mansion of **Yum chaac** the rain god.

THE TEMPLE OF THE WARRIORS OR OF THE THOUSAND COLUMNS

This enormous building is known by these two names. Its restoration was begun in 1924, sponsored by the Carnegie Institution, and carried out by experienced specialists under the direction of Sylvanus G. Morley and Earl H. Morris, among others.

The restorers selected this structure because its size seemed to indicate certain importance; at the time, it looked rather like the two mounds that can be seen on the eastern side of this plaza.

During restoration, this complex of buildings seemed to take shape as if by magic. Because the rectangular columns facing west (the front of the building) and the front row of columns on the southern platform, have relief-carvings on all sides of richly dressed, obviously important figures, and because most of them are holding lances, this structure received the name of Temple of the Warriors. The architects of that era, built the pyramid first and then added the rectangular columns along the front; perhaps later adding the series of cylindrical columns that extend southward and end at a small mound. At right angles to this, another colonnade runs about 200 meters eastwards, towards another unrestored mound. Embedded in the south wall of the Temple, alongside the colonnade that runs east-west, is a long masonry bench with a throne or dais-like projection, and carved figures of various warriors, holding lances, and moving in single file from the ends towards the front where a container for offerings is shown. Feathered serpents are carved along the cornice that finishes off this small dais.

Some researchers believe that this colonnade supported a palm-thatched roof, because during restoration, none of the stones characteristic of the false arch were found; it seems absurd, however, that a building of such seeming importance would have such a rustic addition. Moreover, angular palm-thatched roofs resting on rows of columns would certainly have leaked water. Perhaps the roof was flat, in the Toltec manner, since the majority of these columns still have the capitals that would have supported the wooden beams.

The fronts of the superimposed platforms of the Temple of the Warriors

Detail of the carvings around the superimpoused platforms at the Temple of the Warriors.

Temple of the Warriors. Aerial photo courtesy of José López Nájera.

are decorated in bas-reliefs showing seated figures, each holding a lance in the defense position. The first figure is facing a jaguar sitting on its haunches; the second is facing an animal unknown in the fauna of this region, for it looks like a bear; and the third is facing an eagle; all three animals are holding hearts in their claws. These bas-reliefs are repeated in the same order around the whole pyramid, and on three levels. No decorations were found around the last platform as this section had sustained the worst damage.

Chacmool. Photo by the Author

Behind the mound located about 200 meters south, is another colonnade running east and built on a platform. There are 50 columns in all; the four in the center have carvings of figures, each with uniquely different facial features; some of the colors in which they were painted can still be seen. Behind this edifice on the north side), there is a depression, quite a few meters deep, that was one of the many quarries from which stone was taken for the construction of the nearby buildings. There is also another larger mound with columns, but it has not been restored.

The only stairway at the Temple of the Warriors has 36 steps that are 10 meters wide. Resting on the uppermost platform, are two chambers, together measuring 18 meters long and 9 meters wide, with high rectangular columns decorated with figures in relief. The height of the walls and the columns indicate that the roofs were not angular, but flat, like the Toltec roofs.

In front of these two chambers is a reclining idol known as "chacmool", a Maya word meaning "red claw" (**chac** meaning red and **mool** claw). Present-day Mayas still use this word when speaking of the jaguar.. This idol, like all the others found at Chichén Itzá, has a carved stone plate lying across its stomach that it seems to be holding in his hands; it is believed that incense burners were placed on this plate during religious ceremonies as well as containers with offerings. During excavations, twelve of these idols were found in this northern sector and one in the southern sector; all are in the same reclining position, but have different facial features.

The wide entrance that gives access to these two chambers is guarded by two beautiful columns carved to resemble serpents. The enormous heads of these reptiles, carved out of a solid piece of rock, measure 1.75 meters long, 80 cms wide and 1 meter high; only their forked tongues are separate components. The rectangular columns form the bodies of the serpents, with the rattles projecting upwards at right angles and decorated with crests of feathers. One curious thing about these serpents is that both have small horns on their heads; however, the only snakes that have heads like these are the horned vipers (Cerastes), living in the desert regions of Africa.

At the back of the second chamber, there is a platform or dais with a surface area of 8 square meters, at a height of 75 cms from the floor, and formed by flat stones resting on 19 small idols called atlantes. This platform many have been used as an altar or throne.

On the outside corners of these chambers are sculptures of three large masks, one above the other, each with a long nose resembling the trunk of an elephant. These masks are repeated in the center of the north and south sides; on the front of the building, they flank the entrance door.

Researchers have identified these strange faces as **Yum chaac**, the rain god. Between the masks, are serpents heads with open mouths from which emerge human faces; this has suggested bringing man into the world, and therefore, it is believed that serpents were the symbols of life and fertility. Each of these serpents, in turn, emerges from the mouth of another animal decorated with leaves that look like corn leaves, and with the feet and claws of a bird. These sculptures have been interpreted as an allegory on the origin of life, as represented by the animal kingdom, the plant kingdom and man.

On the front corners of this platform, are twelve hollow stone cones that were used to hold their standards or flags; the same purpose was served by the two idols at the top of the stairway, which have a hole cut through their clasped hands, and through which the flag staff was inserted.

THE BURIED TEMPLE OF CHACMOOL

During restoration work, it was discovered that the MayaToltecs had built an earlier temple on this site; and it was very carefully explored. The base of this building rests almost at the level of the plaza, and is supported by three superimposed platforms, each smaller than the one beneath, and very similar to those of the Castillo. Two chambers were found, with angular roofs supported by walls and columns. Each chamber is 15 meters

Detail of the facade (northeast side) of the Temple of the Warriors. On the corner of the building and on the right are theree mask of Chaac, the rain god. In the center, a serpent with open mouth from which a human head emerges. Photo by A. Cabrera, courtesy of Irma Cantón de Cárdenas.

ong and 6 meters wide. The columns are still well-preserved. and one can eadily see figures elegantly dressed in skirts, some appearing to be made of aguar skins, others of colored cotton. Some of the skirts are short, stoping above the knees, while others reach the ankles. All are wearing sandals richly adorned with tassels and other ornaments. Many of the figures re wearing feather-crested headdresses and are holding scepters an indication f high-ranking officials.

Various offerings were found in these chambers, with one of the most mportant being a turquoise mosaic found in a stone urn and restored by a apanese jeweler. This mosaic was taken to México City's Museum of Anhropology. Other items found were: flint tools, jade jewelry, sea shells, tall cylindrical vases and an incense burner in the shape of a pipe 50 cms long, these last two were fashioned of red clay in the style of Toltec ceramics; they can be seen at the Archeological Museum in Mérida; the pipe is very similar to a pipe found in the Michoacan culture.

There used to be colored murals on the walls, but as the stucco has fallen off, they have disappeared. One mural depicted a fishing village on the sea shore, with thatched-roof huts similar to those still used today by the Maya peasants. Figures of both men and women were shown going about their various chores, fishermen were paddling their canoes and various species of marine life were swimming in the water.

Mural from the subestructure of the Temple of the Warriors; no longer in existence. Reproduction from Official Guidebook to Chichén Itzá I. N. A. H.

Another mural showed a scene of human sacrifices in which a person was lying on a table, shaped like a feathered serpent, and being held down by two others, one holding the hands and one the feet. The executioner was standing over the victim with a flint ax, ready to open the chest, take out the heart and offer it to the gods. In the second chamber, is another chacmool, which is why this buried structure is named the Temple of Chacmool, or substructure to the Temple of the Warriors.

THE MARKET

The construction that lies on the southern edge of this great plaza is known as The Market. This complex was restored in 1933, by the Carnegie Institution of Washington, D.C.

This enormous platform which is 80 meters long and 9.80 meters wide, was at one time partially covered by roofs supported on the south, east and west sides by walls and along the front by 36 columns. The remainder had been left in the open. These columns are alternately cylindrical and parallelepipedal. To climb this 2-meter high platform, the ancient Mayas built an 11-step stairway in the middle, 19.20 meters wide, plus two other stairways on the east and west ends.

The Market. Photo by the author.

Attached to the back wall and to the left of the entrance door, is a small altar, 3 meters long and 2.20 meters deep, decorated with figures in relief walking from the ends towards the center; their hands are tied to a rope that in turn, ties them to each other. From the east wall to what remains of the corridor, runs a built-in, masonry bench, broken only by this small altar and a wide doorway that leads to a rectangular patio enclosed by high walls.

In the center of the patio is a shallow pond surrounded by tall columns which are so thin it seems impossible that they would have supported angular roofs, particularly at that height.

Speculation is that the Mayas used this building as a marketplace, where on certain days of the month, they exchanged products in accordance with pre-established rules.

Tradition tells us that the Mayas used the following as currency: cocoa beans, carved stone beads, sea shells of different shapes and sizes and other objects of conventional value. It is believed that the pond in the center served to keep aquatic animals alive, such as sweet water fish, turtles and others.

Along the east side, various annexes were added to this building at later dates; these roofs were also supported by walls and colonnades.

THE STEAM BATH

About 100 meters to the east and slightly northwards from the Market, there is a structure known as the Steam Bath. This T shaped building has a front chamber that is 16 m. long and 3 m.wide. Its angular roofs were supported by walls on the north, east and south sides and by 4 columns along the front. Inside, on the north side, is a partially destroyed, low platform and on the south side, another lower one. Along the left, another platform was built in at a height of 1 meter, measuring 1.90 meters long and 1.85 meters deep. The remaining space along that side is occupied by a long masonry bench. The rear chamber, which forms the vertical part of the T, connects with the front chamber through a rectangular opening so low that it can only be crawled through. When this rear chamber was completely roofed, it was almost impossible to see out of it; its ventilation consisted of two round windows set high on the north and south walls. At the back (east side), is an oven measuring 1.50 by 2 meters; its entrance was semicircular, until a short while ago; it seems to have been recently destroyed by irresponsible visitors. The curious thing about this arch was

Steam bath or Sweat House. Photo by the Autor.

hat it was built with the technique of the roman arch, quite different from
ll the others; it is not known if this was done by the ancient Mayas or by
he restorers.

Behind this building, the Mayas added a stairway that almost reaches the
evel of the roof, plus other small annexes; one of these is only a low
mound.

The late, Yucatecan archeologist Manuel Cirerol Sansores, believed that
his was not a steam bath but a crematorium. We do know that the Mayas
remated their dead, particularly the nobles, as earthenware urns containing
ashes and bits of charred bones were found on excavating certain buildings.

THE OSARIO OR TOMB OF THE HIGH PRIEST

This pyramid, at present quite deteriorated, was first explored at the turn
of the century by Edward Herbert Thompson. He named it "The Sepulcher
of the High Priest" because inside, he found five superimposed tombs.
Other tourist guidebooks call it the "Osario" or Ossuary and, erroneously,
mention seven tombs.

In shape it resembles the Castillo or Temple of Kukulcan, as it has var-
ous superimposed platforms, each smaller than the one below. The top
platform measures 13.60 meters from east to west and 12.60 meters from
north to south, and is the base for a small temple, the roof of which had
been supported by walls and four columns; the two front columns form the
bodies of enormous feathered serpents with their heads resting on the floor.
The inside columns are carved with very elaborately dressed figures. The
upper portion of the left column is carved with 12 hieroglyphs (also some
numbers, as numbers 2, 3 and 11 are clearly recognizable). The glyphs on
he right-hand column are quite eroded. The center chamber had been surrounded by another narrower one, measuring 1.95 meters wide, with a door
n each of the four sides, leading to the top of each stairway. The main
stairway, which faces east, still has one of the enormous serpents' heads
which decorated the base of the stairs. As we have said before, Thompson
purchased the Chichén Itzá "hacienda" which the Spaniards had built with
stones from the ruins: the property covered the whole archeological site,
plus several kilometers of surrounding land.

Upon exploring the floor of the above described chambers, Thompson
noticed a flagstone in the center which he thought might be the entrance to
a hiding place; it was carefully lifted with the help of local Mayas. Much
to his surprise he found a six-sided pit the walls of which were covered with
flat stones, some of which had small, 5-cm wide projections jutting out at
regular intervals serving as ladder to climb down to the bottom. At a depth

of about 4 meters, he found a human skeleton in fetal position, quite deteriorated and covered with dust and powdery lime. The skeleton was surrounded by offerings of ceramics, most of them broken because of material that had fallen on them. On cleaning out the bottom of this pit, he found another flagstone, similar to the one above; this was the cover to a second tomb. The human skeleton found in it was much better preserved. The third tomb produced offerings of a handful of copper bells, tarnished with age.

In the next tomb, that is, the fourth, he found an offering of a pretty bead necklace made of rock crystal, finely cut and polished. At that point, he realized he had reached ground level and so thought there could be nothing further down, as this land is very stoney and the Mayas of that time had no tools for digging. Nevertheless, looking the area over carefully, he discovered an entrance that had been walled up with hardened ashes; he managed to dislodge this with his feet. He found a short staircase going down to a small, underground chamber covered with ashes. With the help of his Maya workers, he extracted the ashes in baskets hauled up by ropes and found a few jade pieces among the debris. Once the chamber had been emptied, the intrepid Thompson entered it with his four helpers; the heat was suffocating because of lack of ventilation. He discovered a stone slab in the floor which jutted up above the floor level; this was lifted and a dark passage was discovered from which a strong air current flowed. It was another tomb with a human skeleton lying stretched out in an east-west direction. This was the most important tomb of all, it contained rich offerings such as magnificent, multi-colored pottery objects; a large alabaster vase, covered with drawings, but split down the middle, inside of which he found artistically carved jade pieces; and inside a large and highly-polished conch shell, he found two pieces of mother-of-pearl, apparently the eyes of a face engraved on the shell. Other mother-of-pearl pieces of lesser quality fell apart at the touch because of the effects of humidity and acidity.

Thompson described his findings only briefly at that time, the Mexican government was demanding $1,300,000 as compensation for the objects removed from the Sacred Cenote and other sites at Chichén Itzá, but even after a protracted lawsuit, nothing was ever collected.

Thompson believed that an important priest was buried in this underground chamber, and that the other tombs belonged to his acolytes or servants, accompanying him to the next life. Perhaps the hieroglyphic inscriptions on the columns of this temple, will explain the purpose of these enigmatic tombs.

The oft-cited Cirerol Sansores indicated he had been told that the underground tomb was connected to the Castillo; this he did not believe. The author of this book did some investigating of his own among the people that live in the area. Through Francisco Burgos (one of the men who had worked on this archeological site), I found out that in the walls of the Xto-loc Cenote, are two caverns: one running westwards, towards the Osario; and the other southwards, towards the Observatory. Burgos and I agreed to explore them. We entered the one heading towards the Osario (not without considerable danger of being bitten by snakes, scorpions, wasps and other poisonous creatures). At first, we could walk standing up, then we had to bend over; soon we were on hands and knees and finally crawling on our stomachs (and all with only a small flashlight). About 200 meters into the caverns, we reached a section in which we could stand up again. We were in a chamber with a vaulted roof, about 2.40 meters high. At that moment, we heard the echo of tourists' voices from above; it appeared that the top of the vaulted roof had been closed off with stones and mortar. From this vaulted chamber, a passage continued northwards, more or less in the direction of the Castillo. We entered it, bending over, but after about 20 meters, we decided to go back, afraid that the batteries would die on us and we would be trapped in darkness.

From this mini-exploration, we might speculate that perhaps the Mayas built these tombs there so that the spirit of this most important person would have access to the outside. Maybe the cave passage running north does connect to the Castillo; and maybe the other passage running south from this same Cenote does connect to the Observatory. Perhaps that is why those buildings were built at those particular locations.

DESCRIPTION OF THE CENTRAL GROUP

The buildings in the Central Group are the oldest at Chichén Itzá, th being the section where its founders first settled in A.D. 514.

When the Toltecs arrived, they joined the Mayas in this sector, as ca be seen by their architectural influence on some of the buildings.

THE RED HOUSE OR CHICHAN CHOB

About 150 meters south of the Osario, is one of the betterpreserve buildings of this.group, sitting atop a 4-meter high platform, and reache by a stairway 7 meterswide and with 17 narrow steps.

The building is 15 meters long and 8 meters wide. Inside, it is divide into two sections, with roofs built in the classical style of the Maya arch The rear section is subdivided into three small chambers, each having a doe leading to the front section; the latter has three entrance doors, proportion ately spaced. Still in place are some of the original wooden beams whic the Mayas embedded in the walls of the angular arches. These crossbeam were probably used as supports for the scaffolding during roof construction as various are found at different levels; they may have been left in place an used to hang up the nobles' headdresses and vestments.

On the back wall of the front chamber (over the level of the doors), is frieze with mysterious hieroglyphs that runs the length of the chamber.

It was named the "Red House", because the front chamber, to a heigh of little over a meter, was painted red and bordered by a narrow band o blue, remnants of which do not exist today.

Its second name, "Chichan Chob" was given by the Mayas of the Deca dent Period, after it had been abandoned. Some tourist guidebooks indicat that **chichan chob** means small holes, but the Maya-Spanish dictionary states that **chichan** means small, and **chob** plate, thus small plate. It i disconcerting not to have logical reasons for names perhaps the followin; is an explanation: it is almost certain that when Chichén Itzá was aban doned, some of its inhabitants moved to the neighboring village of Pisté these people kept coming back to the ruined buildings of their ancestors and perhaps, on one occasion, found a small plate in that building. Then every time they returned there they would say, "We're going to the buildin; where we found the small plate." With the passage of time, the name stuck.

These were the conditions of the Casa Colorada (Red House) or Chichan Chob, according to the famous artist Frederick Catherwood.

The Red house or Chichan Chob. photo by the Autor.

Along the roof, this building has double ornamentation; the front portion, flush with the wall, has what is called a false façade, and on it the ancient Mayas placed three, very similar masks of Chaac, the rain god, with a human face between the eyes. The back portion, flush with the front wall of the second chamber, has a higher, ornamental superstructure known as the "crestería" or stone crest. Both these additions were used to make the buildings look higher than they actually were; they also compensated for the differences in height between two or more buildings close to each other.

Behind this building (on the east side), a small ball court was built at about the time of the Toltecs' arrival. One can still see the bole in whic the stone ring had been embedded, and at ground level, the platform con mon to all ball courts. The relief-carvings of the players, with uniform similar to those of the large ball court in the Northern Group, are still di tinguishable, with the exception that here, there are only eight players Four are carved on the low platform on the east side, and four on the opp site platform; they are facing each other in groups of two. The rubb along the back belongs to the wall that used to be there.

Four small ball courts, aside from the large one already described, ha been found at Chichén Itzá: three in the Northern Group, plus the one ju mentioned.

THE HOUSE OF THE DEER

About 80 meters northeast of the Red House, is another structure sitti atop a platform, and at practically the same level as the former; this buil ing is facing south. Its architecture is similar to that of the Red House, a it is assumed that they were built at about the same time. The front use to have a wide stairway, but only remains of it can be seen today.

This building has two chambers, also with angular roofs; one of the chambers has had a mural depicting various deer; thus, the name "TI House of the Deer".

THE CARACOL OR OBSERVATORY

This interesting and beautiful structure is known by both these names It is one of the most important buildings at Chichén Itzá, and at differe times, additions were built on and various remodeling jobs were done.

After the conquest, many adventurers and explorers visited this place One of these was John Lloyd Stephens, a U.S. diplomat, who first arrive in 1841, together with the talented architect and artist, Frederick Cathe wood.

Stephens called this structure the "Caracol" (or Snail) when describi it, because inside the tower was a narrow spiral staircase leading up to small round chamber, found partially in ruins. The name of "Observator is used because the building is round and looks like a modern-day observ tory; it also has a window on the west side of the small, upper chamb and at sunset on the equinoctial days (March 21 and September 22) tl shadow made by the exterior southwest corner is cast on the opposite insi

The Caracol or Observatory, prior to restoration (west side) Photographed in 1889 by Henry N. Sweet; published in "Maudsley's Biología Centrali-América", Vol. III, plate 21b. Taken from the book "El Caracol of Chichén Itzá".

The Caracol or Observatory, after restauration. Photo by the Autor.

edge of this window. Also on March 21, at moonset, the shadow made by the exterior northeast corner is cast on the opposite inside corner or edge of this same window. Also in this halfruined chamber, are two small, square holes (it is assumed that originally there were six, evenly distributed around the perimeter), from which the Maya astronomers observed the movements of the stars and other celestial bodies. From photographs taken prior to restoration, it can be seen that the building was densely covered with vegetation and almost 60% of it lay in ruins.

The work done by the restorers is truly admirable; using the stones scattered throughout the building, they were able to rebuild and restore it to its present condition, although some portions simply could not be put back together again.

Many people directed the restoration work under the sponsorship of the Carnegie Institution of Washington: it was started by O.G. Rickeston, Jr., in 1925; the following year, Eric S. Thompson was in charge; from 1927 to 1931, work continued under the supervision of Dr. Karl Ruppert, with a temporary interruption in 1928. Others that contributed their valuable knowledge, expertise and advice were: Dr. Sylvanus G. Morley, Dr. Morris Steggeda, Harry E.D. Pollock, and John S. Bolles, as well as many local and national authorities.

During restoration, it was discovered that originally, the circular tower rested on the rectangular platform, the base of which is at ground level, and which has the following dimensions: 51.5 meters from east to west, 66.90 meters from north to south and a height of 8 meters.

To reach the upper part of the first platform, the Mayas used a stairway with four steps; the first three were 1 meter wide, and the last 90 cms. These ended at a 35-meter long platform or landing; from this landing, another stairway went up, 26.50 meters long, with 18 narrow steps. These stairs were subsequently covered with another stairway with the same number of steps, but wider, making the stairway longer and the landing narrower.

These explorations also uncovered the fact that a circular platform had been added around the tower, with the top of this round platform level with the floor of the tower's chambers. At the base of this platform, a circular bench was added, 75 cms high and 1.10 meters wide. The bench ends before reaching the west, or front door (which is where the landing is), leaving a space 1.20 meters wide. The edges of the stairs to both the first and second platforms are decorated with rattlesnakes, intertwined and reversed so that the head of one serpent lies next to the rattles of the other. These serpents are scaled, which indicates that this building was erected prior to the arrival of the Toltecs, who introduced the feathered serpents at Chichén Itzá. This refutes the theory expounded by some researchers, who believe that this building belongs to the Postclassic Period, only because some round buildings are also found at Calixtlahuaca, Toluca and other sites that were influenced by the Toltecs.

At a later date, the Mayas covered the circular platform and bench with another rectangular platform that has a parapet 56 cms high and 84 cms wide. On top of the parapet, evenly spaced and embedded, are stone carvings of 25 human heads, each with different features; these heads are hollow on top and face outwards; it is believed that they were used as incense burners during religious ceremonies.

In the round part of the building, there are two concentric, circular chambers around a masonry core containing a spiral staircase up to the windowed chamber already described. The outside chamber is 1.25 meters wide and its angular vault rises to a height of 7.50 meters; the inside chamber is narrower, being 1.15 meters wide and 6.25 meters high. There are four entrances to the outside chamber, each 1.90 meters high and 1.04 meters wide; these doors are 17. off from precisely facing in the direction of the four cardinal points. The doors to the inside chamber are 2 meters high and 75 cms wide; they are not exactly centered between the doors leading outside.

During excavations, in the niche that divides the stairway to the second platform, a stela or stone block was found, split in two; it is 1.75 meters long, 83 cms wide and 38 cms thick. Its front surface contains reliefs of 84 hieroglyphs and its periphery 48 more, for a total of 132. This writing in stone is the longest found at Chichén Itzá; but in spite of the clarity of the carvings, it has been impossible to decipher a date because the position of the calendrical hieroglyphs does not follow the known order, leaving the chronologists stumped.

A circular stone was also found; it is 73 cms in diameter, 24 cms thick, and has a projecting bracket or arm for embedding. On the front of this stone, are relief carvings of twelve figures who appear to be priests because of their clothing and reverential postures. Along the top, three are walking towards the center to meet another three coming in the opposite direction. The other six are carved in the same way along the bottom. The circular, outside portion is covered in glyphs. This stone is now on exhibit at the Archeology Museum in Mérida. Numerous fragments of human bones, mostly children's, were also unearthed from this niche, buried at a depth of 48 cms. In the space between the circular platform attached to the tower, and the rectangular platform, two grey pottery vessels were found; one, slightly broken on top, contained ashes and charred bone fragments, plus two pieces of obsidian, 10 and 11 cms long. The second was larger, and also contained ashes and bone fragments, but no offerings. The bones that had not been incinerated were found close by, and consisted of 14 skull fragments (some almost whole), plus 18 lower jaws (some whole, some broken); these bones were found to belong to men, women and children.

In another section, more bones were found: 48 fragments of adult skulls, 20 femurs, 16 tibias, some radial bones and shoulder blades, 185 molars and teeth; in addition, 19 small blocks with hieroglyphs on them, some stone idols and many other objects too numerous to list.

OBSERVATORY ANNEX

In front of the Observatory (towards the western corner), an annex had been built that rested on a platform measuring 2.30 meters high, 19.40 meters long and 13.90 meters wide; its roof had been supported by walls and columns. Towards the back, is a masonry bench, 60 cms high and 1.45 meters wide; there are some niches along the bottom of it. To reach this platform, stairs had been built with narrow steps. This platform was subsequently enlarged, and the stairs replaced with others, the edges of which were decorated with feathered serpents. This group and its columns indicate that this annex was added at the beginning of the Postclassic or Toltec Period.

THE TEMPLE OF THE WALL PANELS

This building is located about 80 meters southeast of the Observatory. Its construction shows strong Toltec influence which is easily recognized by its colonnades and characteristic slope. It was attached to a small pyramid about 6 meters high, on which lie the foundations of two chambers. The first is 7.50 meters long and 1.70 wide; the second is so narrow (only

Temple of the Wall Panels. Photo by the Autor.

55 cms wide) it looks more like a closet with a door in front. The wide entrance of the front chamber consists of two cylindrical. columns in the center and two narrow wall panels on the sides.

To reach these chambers, the Maya-Toltecs built a stairway down the front which used to reach ground level, but when the Temple of the Wall Panels was added, parts of this stairway and portions of the body of the small pyramid were removed.

The name "Temple of the Wall Panels" comes from the panels carved into the north and south exterior walls showing figures of animals, people and other motifs. Among the animals represented, are birds, jaguars, monkeys, fish and serpents that were painted in bright colors. These relief panels cover a surface area of 2 meters long by 1 meter wide.

Some years ago, a local archeologist mistook the tail part of a feathered serpent for the figure of a horse on the south panel. It is hard to see now because the head and part of the tail have been destroyed. As there were no horses in America in those days, the archeologist assumed that it was a Peruvian llama the idea having been brought here by itinerant travellers; however, from a drawing made after its restoration, it is clearly the body of a serpent with long feathers, particularly along the tail.

This building consists of a chamber 18 meters long and 7 meters wide; it had been roofed by three angular naves, the shapes and dimensions of which are easily visible. These naves were supported by walls and columns; six inside and four in front, two of which no longer exist; however, one can still see the capitals on which the thick, wooden beams rested, which in turn, supported the heavy angular roofs.

In an effort to show the original thickness of the beams, mostly destroyed by the weather, the restorers replaced them with similar pieces of wood.

A long, masonry bench is attached along the inside walls of the north, east and south sides.

To reach the small pyramid located in back, another stairway, 7 meters wide, was built along the front, level with the roof of this "Temple of the Wall Panels" and with the floor of the small pyramid's chambers.

To support these steps, a wall was added between the central columns, and between this wall and the solid fill, a narrow passage was left with a Maya arch or vault.

Restoration of this building was paid for by Dr. Francis I. Proctor and his wife (both U.S. citizens) as a sign of their love and admiration for the Maya Culture.

THE "'IGLESIA" OR CHURCH

About 100 meters south of the Temple of the Wall Panels is an interesting building which the Spanish religious leaders named the "Iglesia",

The "Church" as it looked when Catherwood visited Chichén Itzá with Mr. Stephens. This buiding and the east wing of the Nunnery were found in good conditions.

The Iglesia or Church. Photo by the Autor.

possibly because of stories they were told upon arriving on the Peninsula; they were led to believe that vestal virgins went there to pray to the gods prior to being sacrificed in the Sacred Cenote. Unfortunately, once a name has been given to a place or a building, it is almost impossible to change it, no matter how inadequate or absurd. The architecture of this building is in the Puuc style, being decorated with reliefs from the level of the doors to the top. Its base is 11 meters long, 4 meters wide and 8 meters high. Actually, it seems to be too small in relation to its height, having additional ornamentation set above and along the front of the roof consisting of three large masks of the rain god, each of a different size. This additional ornamentation is called a false façade, if it is placed along the front; if it rests on the back portion of the roof, it is called a "cresteria" or stone crest.

Along the front, above the door, this building has three more masks of Chaac, the rain god; one in the center, and one on each end; there are three more along the back wall, placed the same way. Along the front, on the left between the Chaac masks, are relief figures of two, headless persons sitting cross-legged; the first on the left has a bee on his back, and the second has a snail on his back; these have been named "the bee man" and "the snail man". On the right, facing in the opposite direction, is "the turtle man" and "the armadillo man". Because they are four figures, some researcher assumed that they represent the four Bacabes, secondary gods of dread, who support the heavens from the four cardinal points, according to Maya mythology. It should be noted that all the rain gods in this sector, have lowered eye-lashes.

The Mayas did not use windows in their buildings, instead they left openings in the walls of the chambers, almost at door level. The only exceptions to this are: the House of the Seven Dolls in Dzibichaltún, the tower of the Observatory here, the tower of the Palacio at Palenque, and possibly, one or two other buildings in this Maya region.

This building is noticeably leaning outwards, that is, its base is narrower than its top. This can also be seen in the Observatory's tower and in almost all other Maya constructions.

THE NUNNERY

Only two meters southwest of the "Iglesia" or Church, is a group of buildings, with the one called the "Nunnery" standing out for its size and complexity. This name was given by the Spanish religious leaders who visited here after the Conquest.

This building was added to and remodeled at different times. Originally, it consisted of nine rectangular chambers joined by common walls, three chambers in a row. Each group of three has connecting doors in the middle, and the chambers on each end have doors to the outside. Another chamber was later added, perpendicular to the wall of the three facing east. It has the most beautiful façade of all the buildinqs at Chichén Itzá, its architecture reflecting the Chenes style, as reliefs totally cover the front of the building.

Above the door on the east side, is a lintel carved with hieroglyphs which may some day explain something about the building. This door also

The Nunnery as found by the artist Catherwood.

East side of the Nunnery at Chichén Itzá. Photo by the Autor.

represents an enormous mouth: the stylized lips are short lines that look like folds, the teeth are hooks which are mostly broken off, and around these the gums are molded in stucco. Above the mouth is a high-relief of an idol sitting on its legs, with arms crossed, and surrounded by an arch that forms a niche. This high-relief, in turn, is outlined by two serpents, the bodies of which are zig-zag lines.

Catherwood shows us the state of preservation in which he found the "Church" and the Nunnery.

Aereal view of the Nunnery and the "Church" As it looks now. Photo courtesy of Mr. José López N'...

Some specialists believe that this figure represents the "Goddess of orn", probably because of the stylized ears of corn on either side. The reainder of the decorations of this façade, are twelve masks of the rain god, it with moustaches; across the forehead, each has a line of corn kernels, iding at either end in ears of corn. One can still see part of the original ucco with vestiges of red and blue, as part of the many colors it must ive had.

Along the cornice, is a long, broken line made of precisely cut, dentate ones, forming the body of an ondulating .and stylized rattlesnake which ns around the building, ending with the rattles at the far north side. Un-r the cornice on this same side, is a row of five Chaac masks, each has a iman face in the space between the eyebrows. Below these, is a series of dividually crafted crosses, joined together to form a lattice. Slightly be-w the level of the entrances, is a frieze that looks like a long ribbon with ort folds.

Upon exploring the west side, it was found that close to the wall of the st three chambers, a high platform had been built with a small temple on p. At a later date, this platform was covered by another larger and slight-higher one, on top of which various chambers were built; some of the one lintels have hieroglyphic carvings on them. This upper part is also the Chenes style of architecture. Subsequently, this second platform was tended at both ends and to support its enormous weight, it was necessary fill in the three last chambers on the west side of the ground floor. The ason why the two central chambers of the next row of six were also filled is unknown; the chambers on each end remained connected by a central ssageway.

Another annex, of Toltec influence, was built on to this temple in back putheast corner), forming a small rectangular patio with the rest of the mplex. About three meters east of this pomplex is another building with o chambers; its façade is ornamented with masks of Chaac and it is in the iuc architectural style.

In front and to the left of the "Nunnery", other chambers were built; eir Toltec influence is easily recognizable in the sloped foundation and lumns. This group forms a small rectangular patio.

THE AKAB DZIB OR HOUSE OF DARK WRITING

About 200 meters to the east of the Nunnery is a structure known by its aya name of Akab Dzib. The name of this building comes from the aya words akab meaning night, and dzib writing, interpreted, however, as ark writing", because on the south wall of the second inside chamber is a stone lintel with hierogliphic carvings, the meanings of which are unknown. On the underside of this lintel is another carving showing the figure of an important person sitting on a throne with the left leg twisted under the thigh, and wearing a headdress with a showy crest of feathers; one hand is taking food or offerings out of a basket. Other hieroglyphs partially surround this figure. Because of the fine quality of these carvings, which sharply contrast with the simple decorations on the façade consisting of two cornices, one with three bands along the center, the other with two bands along the top it is believed that this lintel did not originally belong to this building, but that it was taken there at a later date from some other building.

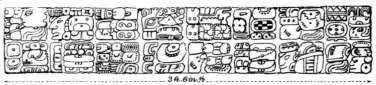

In the upper part are gliphs carved on a stone lintel of the Akab Dzib building. The figure and gliphs of the lower part of the same lintel are also carved in bass relief. Catherwood print.

The dimensions of the Akab Dzib are as follows: 54 meters long, 16 meters wide and 6 meters high, with 16 empty chambers, plus others that were filled in with masonry. Its configuration and layout show that it was built in stages; possibly, these chambers were used as living quarters by persons of high rank, or they may have been used as offices.

In some of the chambers on the west side, the ancient Mayas left red paint imprints of their hands on the stucco of the angular roofs. These imprinted hands on roofs and walls, have also been found in the buildings of other cultures, but what their true purpose was is unknown. In the case of the Mayas, it is said that they symbolize the hands of the high priest, Itzamná, founder of Chichén Itzá.

No kitchens or sanitary facilities have been found in Maya buildings; perhaps these were located in the outskirts.

Some meters east of the Akab Dzib, there is an enormous, funnel-shaped depression, covering about one-and-a-half hectares; its central portion measures about 15 meters. This depression was one of the quarries from which stones were taken for the buildings in the area.

THE XTOLOC CENOTE

About 200 meters east of the Osario or Tomb of the High Priest, is a cenote called "Xtoloc", which is slightly smaller than the Sacred Cenote.

Today, this cenote is totally surrounded and overgrown by dense vegetation, giving it a most impressive appearance - trees are.growing around the edges, and steadfastly hanging on to the sides and hollows of its near vertical walls all the way down to the water level. On the east side a cut was made to form a small platform about 5 meters wide and 4 meters deep. A short distance from this platform, is a ramp that descends to the water's edge, its end facing almost due west. This ramp and platform were built by the ancient Mayas, so that they could walk down to the water and easily fill their vessels. Originally, the ramp had steps in it made of blocks of cut stone; some of these can still be seen.

Before reaching the water's edge, are the two caves which have already been described. About 20 meters northeast of this natural well, one can still make out the foundations of three chambers built on a low platform. These must have had angular arched roofs, because in front of the platform are piles of the triangular stones typical of this type of building, as well as some cylindrical columns that supported these roofs in front.

The two rear chambers are the same, each measuring 5.50 meters long and 1.75 meters wide. The front chamber is the largest, and is 14 meters long and 3.75 meters wide. In the left corner, at the back, are some masonry benches.

At the entrance to the second chamber, are two rectangular columns with relief carvings of figures on every side, now quite eroded. On the outside southern edge of the floor, is a rock with a hole, 60 cms in diamete which leads to a concavity in the shape of a cistern.

As Chichén Itzá must have been densely populated at various time there is little doubt that water consumption was heavy, particularly durin times of drought, and water rationing must have been a necessity so that particular sector of the population would be affected. Water was used n only for human consumption, but also for domesticated animals, cloth washing, cooking, washing of utensils, watering of vegetables and plan both medicinal and ornamental, as well as in preparing the mortar for co struction. It is feasible that this building was used as a control office avoid mayhem and anarchy. Perhaps the governing body handed out toke to the inhabitants, which were redeemed upon having access to the cenot These chambers would also then have been living quarters for the guards.

The name Xtoloc, comes from lizards very common to Yucatán; pe haps, some of these lived by the cenote and thus it was given that name.

In the vicinity of Chichén Itzá, and at distances varying from 1 to kms, more than 15 cenotes have been found. Due to their configurati and depth, the water in these at that time, could only have been taken o by hand using wooden buckets tied to ropes made of plant fiber or resista vines.

THE SOUTHERN GROUP

This sector, which some people still call "Old Chichén", consists of
rious groupings of small and medium sized structures, for the most part
ite destroyed. Some of the buildings are pure Maya architecture, others
ow marked Toltec influence.

TEMPLE OF THE DATE

The first important group is located about one kilometer southeast of
e already described Nunnery. On a small mound about four meters high,
a small square chamber, 2.80 meters long; its roof had been supported by
alls, and along the front (south side), by two anthropomorphous idols,
95 meters tall, called "atlantes"; their features and clothing are authenti-
lly Toltec. These atlantes formed the door posts and across them lies a
rge, stone lintel, with hieroglyphic carvings showing a date equivalent to
D. 879 (according to Goodman, Martinez Hernandez and Thompson), or
D. 619 (according to Spinden). As the Toltec influence did not reach
hichén Itzá until approximately A.D. 987, it has been assumed that this
ne did not originally belong to this building, but that it had been
ought from some previous construction; nevertheless, it continues to be
lled the Temple of the Date. This small building was subsequently added

Atlantes", with Toltec features and clothing, that used to support the
oof of this small structure, now hold up a stone slab carved with
ieroglyphs. Photo by José López Nájera.

to and remodeled.

About 12 meters away from the front of this building, lies one of the 13 chacmools found at Chichén Itzá.

TEMPLE OF THE PHALLIC SYMBOLS

About 80 meters from the Temple of the Date, is a group of rectangular chambers joined in a double row. Three of these, still in good condition, have low, 55-cm platforms which may have been used as benches, beds, altars. Embedded in the walls are phallic symbols, each 25 to 30 cms long and 23 cms in diameter, and from which the temple receives its name. The two chambers on the south side were later filled in with masonry so as to build other chambers on top; the foundations of these still exist.

Various other buildings were added to the patio on the east side of these chambers; those towards the outside had their roofs supported by walls and columns; the reliefs on these columns depict figures similar to the ones found on the colonnade of the Temple of the Warriors. Further back, towards the northeast, are two atlantes, again used as door posts, very similar to the ones at the Temple of the Date. This indicates that these annexes were added during the Postclassic or Toltec Period.

Patio (west side) of the Temple of the Fallic Symbols. Photo by Joel López Nájera.

Towards the south end of this patio, a long chamber was built with an arch, now destroyed. Along the central cornice, at door level, all around the building, and equidistant one from another, are relief-sculptures which some have interpreted as being snails, although they look more like stylized phallic symhols. This group of buildings forms a small quadrangle.

HOUSE OF THE OWLS

Because of the relief carvings of these nocturnal birds on the faces of its columns, this rather ruined little building was given the name of the House of the Owls; it is located about 60 meters south of the small quadrangle described above.

Possibly, this building was used as a consulting office by the "curandero" (witch doctor or healer) who helped the sick or put spells on others. It is known that the Mayas employed these "curanderos" when they wanted a malediction cast on someone because of quarrels or bitter resentments, and the owl (a bird of ill omen) was used as an element in their evil spells.

THE CASTILLO OF OLD CHICHEN

The next important group is located about 500 meters southeast of the Temple of the Date. The most important structure in this sector is a small pyramid, named the Castillo of Old Chichén. It is about 12 meters high, ending in a small platform on which are the foundations of some chambers, the roofs of which were supported by walls and columns which can still be seen in spite of being quite destroyed. The columns are decorated with reliefs among which is an eagle, some serpents and other motifs.

Around this structure are various stone mounds that were chambers, presently in ruins. In some, the Maya arch can be seen; others show similarities to buildings in Tula.

Towards the eastern end of Old Chichén, and about 550 meters away, there are three structures quite close to each other, the first known as the Temple of the Lintel, the second as the Temple of the Four Lintels, and the third as the Temple of the Three Lintels.

TEMPLE OF THE LINTEL

The Temple of the Lintel is a small building with two chambers in ruins; the front chamber had two columns at its entrance; the inside or back one, had a lintel across its door, from whence the name. This lintel, carved with hieroglyphs and numerals, now rests on the floor.

TEMPLE OF THE FOUR LINTELS

This building, also, has two adjoining chambers; the first is 9 meters long and 4 meters wide. On the west side it has two doors or entrances, the lintels of which are beautifully carved with hieroglyphs both on the front and the underside. Another door, toward the south, has a lintel similar to the others, except that in the center there is a relief of a coiled rattlesnake with an open mouth from which emerges a human face. The second chamber, toward the north, measures 4 by 2.40 meters, and connects to the front one by means of an entrance that has the fourth lintel. The reliefs on this one depict a stylized bird with a serpent's neck and head, which some have mistaken for a dragon.

TEMPLE OF THE THREE LINTELS

This is the largest and most beautiful of the buildings in the Southern Group; its architecture is Puuc style and very similar to the buildings at Uxmal. It is 16 meters long, 4.50 meters wide and about 4 meters high. Its façade is decorated with built-in vertical columns, separated by squares that resemble tiles. Above the level of the doors is a frieze of cut stones laid in a zig-zag pattern with triangles in between, going all around the building. At the corners of the building, both up high and at ground level, are masks of the rain god Chaac.

This structure is divided into three chambers of equal size, each with a door leading to the front, and a stone lintel. The lintels of the doors on

Temple of the Three Lintels, in the Southern Group. Photo by the Autor.

each end are carved with various hieroglyphs, while the lintel of the middle door shows marks made with a cutting tool; whether the glyphs were erased by vandals or whether the lintel was replaced with a non-carved one, is not known.

This structure was restored by the archeologists of the Carnegie Institution of Washington, D.C., who transformed a heap of rubble into its present, beautiful shape.

South of the Chichén Itzá "hacienda", and about one kilometer away, is a structure known as the "Hieroglyphic Door Posts"; and northeast of the "hacienda", are other buildings known as: the Columns of Atlantes and Snails, the Sculptured Door Posts, the Cornices of the Birds. the Jaguar Atlantes, the Turtle Atlantes and others. These are not described, because they are almost totally in ruins and of lesser importance.

While walking through these different groups of buildings, and seeing the many stone and earth mounds that were once buildings now lying in ruins it is easy to see how large and important a center Chichén Itzá must have been at the height of its glory.

BIBLIOGRAPHY

Acosta, Jorge R. y Pablo Martínez del Río. **Guía Oficial de Tula**, INAH, México, D. F. 1961.

Arochi, Luis E. **La Pirámide de Kukulkán: su Simbolismo Solar**, Editorial Orión, México, D. F. 1976.

Blom, Franz. **La Vida de los Mayas**, Biblioteca Enciclopédica Popular, No. 25, S. E. P. México, D. F. 1944.

Barrera Vásquez, Alfredo y Silvia Rendón. **El Libro de los Libros de Chilam Balam**, Fondo de Cultura Económica, México, D. F. 1965.

Canto López, Antonio. **Apuntaciones Sobre Mesoamérica**, Mérida, Yucátan, México. 1973.

Cirerol Sansores, Manuel. **Chi Cheen Itsá**, Talleres Gráficos del Sudeste, S. A. Mérida, Yucatán, México. 1957

Cordemex, **Diccionario Maya-Español y Español-Maya**, Ediciones Cordemex, 1980.

Echánove Trujillo, Carlos, **Esas Pobres Ruinas Mayas Maravillosas**, B. Costa-Amic, Editor. Mesones 14, México 1, D. F. 1973.

Folan William, J. **Chichén Itzá**, Ediciones Orto, S. A., Tehuantepec No. 251, México, D. F. 1977.

Jiménez Moreno, Wigberto, José Miranda y María Teresa Fernández, **Historia de México**, ECLASA, Constitución 18, Librería de Porrúa Hermanos, México, D. F. 1967.

Landa, Diego de, **Relación de las Cosas de Yucatán**, Editorial Porrúa, S. A. México, D. F. 1962.

Morley, Silvanus Griswold, **La Civilización Maya**, Fondo de Cultura Económica, México, D. F. 1975.

Molina Solís, Juan Francisco, **Historia del Descubrimiento y Conquista de Yucatán**, Ediciones Mensaje, México, D. F. 1943.

Piña Chan, Román, **Los Antiguos Mayas de Yucatán**, Departamento de Ediciones del INAH-SEP, Cooproducción del Gobierno del Estado de Yucatán, 1978.

Piña Chan, Román, **Informe Preliminar de la Reciente Exploración del Cenote Sagrado de Chichén Itzá**, Serie Investigaciones No. 24, INAH, México, 1970.

Piña Chan, Román, **Chichén Itzá, La Ciudad de los Brujos del Agua**, Talleres Offset Marvi, México 13, D. F. 1980.

Recinos, Adrián, **Popolvuh. Las Antiguas Historias del Quiché**, Biblioteca Americana, Fondo de Cultura Económica, México, D. F. 1947.

Roys, Ralph L. **The Book of Chilam Balam of Chumayel**, University of Oklahoma Press, Norman, Okla., U. S. A. New Edition, 1967.

Sáenz, César, **Boletín del INAH**, Epoca II, México, D. F. July-September 1972.

Solís Alcalá, Ermilo, **Diccionario Español-Maya**, Editorial Yikal Maya Tan, Mérida, Yucatán, México, 1949.

Solís Alcalá, Ermilo (Translator), **Codice Pérez**, Liga de Acción Social, Imprenta Oriente, Mérida, Yucatán, México, 1949.

Thompson, J. Eric S., **The Rise and Fall of the Maya Civilization**, University of Oklahoma Press, Norman, Okla., U. S. A., 1966.

Thompson, J. Eric. S., **Maya History and Religion**, University of Oklahoma Press, Norman, Okla., U. S. A. Third Edition, 1976.

Thompson, Edward Herbert, **People of the Serpent: Life and Adventure among the Mayas**, Capricorn Books Edition, 1965.

This book was printed by
Libros, Revistas y Folletos de Yucatán,
S.A. de C.V.

TELEFONOS: 25 - 78 - 41   Y   25 - 22 - 43
CALLE 35 No. 505 INTERIOR x 62 y 64

In November, 1991.
Mérida, Yucatán, México.